HELPING
CHILDREN
READ

HELPING

CHILDREN

READ

The Paired Reading Handbook
Roger Morgan BA, PhD

A METHUEN PAPERBACK

First published in Great Britain 1986
by Methuen Children's Books Ltd
11 New Fetter Lane, London EC4P 4EE
Copyright © 1986 Roger Morgan

Printed in Great Britain

British Library Cataloguing in Publication Data

Morgan, Roger. *1949–*
    Helping children read: the paired reading
    handbook.
    1. Reading (Elementary)
    I. Title
    372.4   LB1573

    ISBN 0–416–96540–7

To Ruth and Jennifer

CONTENTS

ACKNOWLEDGEMENTS

My first and clearest thanks go to the numerous children and parents who have been the consumers and shapers of paired reading – and who have at times had to tolerate its teething troubles as well as its successes. I am also grateful to the education authorities and to the Heads and staffs of the schools and remedial services who have permitted and assisted my paired reading work, and to the colleagues I have worked with on various paired reading projects in Birmingham, Kent, Cambridge and Oxford. In particular I am indebted to Elizabeth Lyon and Pam Gavin, my co-workers on early studies. I am also grateful to Keith Topping in Kirklees, who has spread paired reading to numerous schools, and has given me free access to his growing collection of paired reading research.

My sincere thanks go to Christopher Falkus, Chairman of Methuen, for suggesting that I write this book and for his always helpful and friendly advice and support. I also owe a debt of gratitude to my wife Helen for both tolerating my writing activities and ensuring that they take place, to my children Ruth and Jennifer as my best critics of paired reading, and to Christine Shrimpton who succeeded in typing the manuscript without paired reading it.

R.M.

PREFACE

I have written this handbook with three key principles in mind. Firstly, that parents can help their children read (and there is plenty of evidence that they can); secondly, that it is better to say exactly *how* one can help, rather than simply giving exhortations about helping; and, thirdly, that if one is trying to improve a child's reading, then one should take the trouble to check whether the child's reading actually is improving.

If you are glancing through this preface before deciding whether to buy the book or to try its method, turn and skim through the first few pages of Chapter Two to discover what paired reading is. Beyond that, the two core pages in the book are the summary of paired reading on page 65, and the checklist on page 78. The rest of the book sets out in detail what to do and describes the theory behind paired reading, ways of checking whether reading really is improving or not, what to do when things go wrong, and the research evidence on the effectiveness of paired reading in helping children read. I have also included a description of related reading techniques, developments in the use of paired reading, and (in Chapter One) a discussion of the key issues about reading and reading problems that are often raised by parents.

The purpose of this handbook is to give all the guidance necessary to start doing paired reading from scratch, whether you are a parent helping your own child at home, or a teacher or headteacher setting up a home/

school reading scheme. With the increase in recent years of parents as well as teachers helping children read, I have aimed the handbook at both parents and teachers.

Paired reading has become the most popular of the specific methods for parents to use in helping children read. It has also become one of the most widely evaluated activities in education. The technique originated in 1974 when I was treating a child for stammering. I was trying to train him to speak fluently by reading aloud with him. As he was also a poor reader, I wondered what this might be doing to his reading. Paired reading was the result of putting together the elements of reading aloud together and a number of well-established learning principles. My initial, very small scale and very tentative studies suggested that paired reading did help children read – and were followed by many teachers and psychologists working with large numbers of children, publishing reports that paired reading works. It is important that researchers other than me, working independently in many schools in Britain (and now abroad), have reported paired reading to be highly effective. I might be accused of being biassed in its favour – others have subjected it to the acid test and vouched that it does help children read.

There are dangers in writing a handbook. The best way to teach someone a technique is to be there in person. A handbook is second best. I have done my best to include most of the advice I need to give to parents at my own paired reading training and monitoring sessions. My apologies in advance to those who come across issues not covered in the book. However, the teachers and psychologists responsible for the widespread research work on paired reading picked up the technique from my early published accounts of it without further explanation from me – so I see no reason why the readers of this handbook should not pick it up and use it just as effectively.

I should like to make two pleas. Firstly, that parents and teachers should agree together on paired reading being used, and discuss together its effectiveness for the child concerned. It is not helpful if school and home are unaware of what 'the other half' are doing. Secondly, instead of just 'hearing the child read', give paired reading a try. If it doesn't work, fair enough – stop it and little is lost. I will however have succeeded if this book helps to lead some children to be able to use and enjoy things that are written, particularly if it enables them to enjoy the process of learning to read into the bargain.

A final point – throughout this book I have referred to the child as 'he' and the parent as 'she'. This is because, like it or not, most children with reading problems are boys, and most of the parents who help their children read at home are mothers. I find 'he or she' awkward to write and read. I did think of describing the children as 'she' and parents as 'he' – but while I wish more fathers helped children read, I do not wish more reading problems onto girls. Suffice it to say that my choice of pronouns fits the majority, and that as a father I've worked on paired reading with my daughters!

Roger Morgan
Oxford
May 1986

ONE: INTRODUCTION – READING AND READING PROBLEMS

The Importance of Reading

Reading, and failure to read, matter immensely. The ability to read is vital to coping at school, in most jobs, and in many aspects of everyday life. Failure in reading is many a child's first experience of being a failure in comparison with others. Poor reading is like living in a country with an unknown language. Everything written, in books, on forms, on notices, doors and street signs is meaningless; or, worse, only bits can be recognized and one never knows whether one has guessed the rest correctly or is possibly making some terrible mistake. People need to be able to read passably well. The written or printed word is the next most common means of getting everyday information after the spoken word, and one might therefore view reading problems as next most serious after hearing problems. Furthermore reading is going to remain vital in the future even with new technologies. Computer screens rely heavily on the written word as the method of communication between people and machines. The importance and unacceptability of serious problems in reading are underlined by the extreme lengths adults will go to in order to cover up an inability to read.

Quite apart from the necessity to read passably well, a great deal of enjoyment is locked up in books, magazines, newspapers and the written instructions involved in so many activities. The child who finds reading difficult simply misses out on so much potential enjoyment. There is not much fun for a 10 year old in the stilted sentences of the Infant's reading scheme while he is missing the more advanced books

13

of his classmates. For parents, the child's learning to read is his biggest hurdle after learning to become clean and dry. The worry of how he or she is doing compared with the others, and conflicting and often vague advice on whether they should try to 'do something about' reading at home or leave it to the teachers, can be major anxieties. For the teacher, poor reading effectively puts the brake on all other areas of a child's educational progress. It needs time that is not available to be spent on remedial work and on trying to get around reading difficulties when working on other studies. All too often a reading problem escalates into rejection of more and more of what schools and education stand for.

The Complicated Written Word

Reading is an incredibly complicated job. It is amazing that children manage to do it. None of us was born with any knowledge of what the black squiggles you are now reading mean. What is worse, reading English is not a simple matter of learning what sounds go with which letters or groups of letters. Some languages are more straightforward; in Welsh, for instance, the same letters always make the sounds (thus the 'LL' sound English speakers find so hard is the same whatever the word). The Germans and French use accents added above or below letters to tell the reader which of a number of possible sounds to make (e.g. é or è in French). In English, we just leave things difficult – the same letters make different sounds in different words (e.g. in *cough* and *dough*, *c*at and *c*ell), and different letters can make the same sound (e.g. *c*at and *k*itten). Sometimes we just have to guess what to say from the setting in which the word appears (e.g. how to say the word 'read' in the two sentences 'did you read this' and 'have you read that') and for good measure we put in silent letters to trip up the unwary (as in the word 'knock'). At least our letters are simpler than the Chinese have to cope with – though even then we complicate matters by using different shapes for the

14

same letter. A, a and ɑ do not look very much alike, handwritten words aren't much like printed words, and 'l' could (in my four year old daughter's view) be a 'big i' or a 'little L'. Then we break all the rules with oddities like 'etc' or '&'.

Using Clues in Reading

Because written words do not always follow a 'one letter — one sound' rule, we all rely on a whole range of clues from the text in our reading. Apart from the basic rules of phonetics (knowing the sounds letters, pairs of letters or groups of letters usually make) which help us to 'sound out' wards, we use the general shape of the words and the sense of the sentence they are in to tell us what they are. As an illustration, part of this paragraph does not make sense as it is printed because of a spelling error, but you know what it is meant to be by using clues of word-shape and the overall meaning of the sentence. Many readers will not have spotted the incorrect spelling at all because they 'got' the word through these clues rather than through phonetics. (Some may have difficulty finding it even now!)

It is important to stress that 'sounding out' is not the only way of 'getting' a word and that often it doesn't work. Children often mis-spell words by writing them as they sound. My 8 year old daughter has just discovered that the only way to read the word 'Colonel' in her book is to ask Dad and remember it. She will be helped to recall it in future if there is the clue of a military flavour in what she is reading.

Equally important, not only do we all use different clues all the time, but it is very likely that each child is different in the precise way his brain works out what a word is. One child may find it easy and helpful to 'blend' letter-sounds into words, while another will find that saying 'w', 'o', 'r', 'd' quickly never somehow magically turns it into 'word' (much to his parents' or teacher's frustration!). Another may have a good memory for words once he is told what they are, but find breaking them into bits a very confusing way of learning them. Yet another may be an expert at 'guessing' only vaguely remembered words from the setting they come in.

Because of the variations, it is not a good idea to pick on only one way of working out what words are, and expecting any child to succeed automatically with that as his only tool. It is better to use a method of helping with reading that encourages successful reading without limiting the child to using only one kind of 'clue' to words. Paired reading is designed to help in this way.

Usual Methods of Teaching Reading

A number of main approaches are used in schools to teach reading, often in one combination or another. There are (at least) three types of approach. Firstly, the 'whole word' or 'look say' approach. In this, the child is encouraged to recognize whole words and later to build them into sentences. This may involve the use of flash cards bearing a word which is shown to the child, accompanied by the teacher saying the word, until he can recognize it. This is the basis of some programmes aiming to teach extremely young children to read their first words. It also lends itself to being used in computer and reading game equipment which can link words and the sound they make. Putting the child straight onto reading whole words and helping him until he can manage a little on his own, and eventually do without help, has been described as like helping him learn to ride a bicycle.

A second main approach teaches children basic rules of reading, often concentrating on the phonetic rules of the sounds letters and combinations of letters make. Although the problem has already been raised that phonetic rules alone are not enough, they do provide a useful 'first line of attack' in working out a word. Teachers following this approach will often use a range of specially designed games to get the rules of reading across (e.g. games involving picking out words with a 'th' sound).

A third line of approach is to introduce children to

reading through simplified reading materials which become gradually more difficult as the child progresses. The material often has built in clues to help the child get the words. The simplest and most common clues are pictures that show what the word underneath says. More subtle clues involve the careful repetition of words once learnt and the use of different colours as prompts (rather like the French use accents as clues to the sounds to make). Most parents and teachers are familiar with reading schemes of progressively more advanced 'readers'. There are also sets of reading cards, reading-rule games, comprehension work and other materials available as reading 'laboratories'.

Paired reading and some simplified versions of it (described later in this book) are beginning to be introduced in some schools with very young beginning readers. Results so far are encouraging and it is important to note that paired reading will not conflict with the traditional types of teaching reading. As an example, paired reading neither relies on use of phonetics, nor does it train the child to 'sound out'. If however, this is the way the child is working out words, then paired reading will encourage him to do this effectively. Vitally important, there does not appear to be any risk attached to using paired reading approaches with even the youngest readers, despite the fact that it is most often used with 'junior' or 'lower secondary' age children.

Reading Ages and Reading Tests

At some stage during their schooldays, most children will have their reading ability tested. Some schools do this regularly, to keep a check on the children's progress. For most children, the testing is done by a teacher, but where reading problems need investigating, the testing may be done by a remedial specialist or by an educational psychologist. In these cases, more complicated tests are likely to be used, assessing various other aspects of reading skill than the basic 'getting the words right' of most tests. The more complex tests are able to show up particular problem areas that need to be worked upon or monitored in the future.

A common type of test used in schools asks the child to read a set piece, perhaps a list of words of increasing difficulty or a series of short 'stories' of increasing difficulty. His reading accuracy is then measured, often simply by counting his mistakes. A gradual increase in difficulty allows the test to be used with children of different ages and different reading abilities. Testing is usually stopped when the child has worked through the increasingly difficult words or passages to the point where his mistakes reach a set level. Extra exercises may be added to this kind of basic test to assess other aspects of reading skill.

Before they were published, most commonly used reading tests were 'standardized'. This means that the new test was given to a very large number of children of different ages, for their scores to be used to compile a table of the average scores achieved by children of each age. After this, whenever a child is tested on such a standardized test his score is looked up in the table to find out the age of child that would normally achieve that score. This is the tested child's 'reading age'. There are other measures of reading ability, but reading age is by far the most commonly used.

The child's reading age (usually in years and completed months) can be compared with his actual or chronological age. In theory, the average reader has a reading age the same as his chronological age. There are however a number of practical problems with reading tests and because of these it is unwise to treat their results as gospel. It is because of these shortcomings that the results are often not given to parents or children themselves without additional comments needing to be made. The shortcomings of reading tests include the problem that, like any other test or examination, their results can be affected by the child's mood or tiredness. The same child may earn different scores on the same test on different occasions, because of factors like these, without any real differences in his reading. There is even a danger that if the same test is used too often, a child may begin to 'learn the test'. Another problem is that many tests are quite old, sometimes using old-fashioned language. Also, they may not be fully appropriate for children with a mother-tongue other than English. Finally, the tests that are available now are not really accurate enough to measure very well small changes in reading skill over a short period of time. This is a problem in using tests to measure the results of short periods of reading tuition.

Despite all these difficulties, tests do remain the most objective method of assessing whether a child is ahead, behind, or average in reading. In evaluating the effectiveness of reading tuition, including paired reading, tests are vital – but their limitations must not be overlooked. They are certainly not the be all and end all of either a child's reading skill or a method's effectiveness.

Other relevant information (such as the child's interest in the written word and his own views on how well he is reading) should always be taken into account.

READING PROBLEMS
Number of Children with Problems
From information in published research studies, between three and ten out of every hundred British schoolchildren have difficulty in learning to read. A large survey of 9 and 10 year old children (carried out on the Isle of Wight) found that 6.6 per cent of these children had reading ages at least two years and four months behind their actual age.

Differences in Reading Ability
The ability to read is not shared out fairly between all children. For some children, it is an easy task, for others it is extremely difficult. These 'individual differences' between children explain as many children having reading problems as they do children with

19

especially good reading skills. There are as many 'below' average' readers as 'above average' ones, and very few children fall precisely at the average. Indeed, it is not very normal to be average at reading! Having problems with reading does not automatically mean that there is some other special reason for the difficulty than the bad luck of having a low share of the reading skills that are around. Most skills and personal characteristics are spread out among children (or adults) – from reading skills to size of feet, musical ability to body weight. Many children will be familiar with this idea, from making graphs or bar charts of the heights, or some other measurement, of children in the class. I had well below the average 'share' of sporting ability when I was at school, and I find it helpful to explain to many boys with reading problems that I am no more 'odd' because of this than they are for having low reading skills. In either case, if it matters, extra coaching is needed to make the best use of the amount of skill there is.

Reading and Other School Work
For many children, reading difficulties are part of a more general difficulty with school work – some children are simply not the type who 'shine' at school. For others (about four per cent of school children) the reading problem is their only real difficulty at school, and they may even 'shine' at other aspects of school work. Unfortunately, because reading is the key to so much else at school, the child whose only real problem is with reading will soon find that this holds him back in everything else.

Those children for whom reading is the only area of difficulty to start with are said to have a 'specific reading difficulty'. Their problems in learning to read are significantly greater than one would expect from their overall ability. Such children are, therefore, not just those with a low 'share' of general ability, but those who find reading *especially* difficult.

When Help is Needed
Reading problems rarely go away of their own accord, and effective additional help is therefore needed. This is not

necessarily highly specialized, although in some cases it may eventually need to be; in most cases, appropriate help from Mum and Dad at home gives a good chance of making progress. Children with a specific reading difficulty are less likely to progress if they are not given extra help than are children whose reading problems are part of overall difficulties with school work.

There is no hard and fast rule on how serious a reading problem should be before extra help should be arranged. As a rule of thumb, I would normally arrange extra help for a child whose reading age on a standard test is two years or more behind his actual age by the time he is 9 or 10. However, two years behind is a far more significant gap for, say, a 9 year old than it would be for a 15 year old, and whether the gap is widening or narrowing as time goes on is far more important than the size of the gap itself. A child whose gap between reading age and chronological age is rapidly widening as he grows older but progresses little in reading is obviously in greater trouble than the child whose gap is remaining the same or closing. To close the gap, the child's reading must be improving faster than normal, since his reading age is catching up with his chronological age.

Provided that parent and child both enjoy it, a technique like paired reading can be used at home to boost progress even where there is far less of a problem than this rule of thumb. Paired reading can even be helpful (again, provided parent and child enjoy doing it) to a child with no reading problems at all, to encourage his or her further development in reading skills.

If paired reading, or another home-based means of help, has already been tried without success, and the child is not progressing in reading with normal classroom support, more specialized assessment should be considered. A more highly structured and individual remedial technique may prove necessary.

Difference Between Boys' and Girls' Reading

Approximately three times as many boys as girls have reading problems. Why boys are more likely to have reading difficulties than girls is an open question – but boys of school age are more prone than girls to difficulty in developing other sorts of skills as well. As an example, boys are more likely than girls to suffer from bedwetting.

Inherited Reading Problems

Difficulty in learning to read tends to run in families. As many as one in every three children with specific reading difficulty has a close relative with the same problem. There is evidence that one can inherit reading problems. Thus the boy or girl finding learning to read a particularly difficult task may have been born with the problem as part of his or her genetic make-up – and may well pass it on to the next generation.

Physical Problems

For some children, reading problems may be the result of a physical problem putting an obstacle in the way of learning to read. Examples are 'glue ear' and defects in eyesight. Where hearing or eyesight problems are suspected, a medical check should be sought. Problems of this type can usually be corrected.

Problems in Coping with Words

As has been said, reading is an extremely complicated task. We do not just learn all the words in the English language and then recognize them when we meet them in a book. Instead, reading is a mixture of recognizing familiar words, and of rapid detective work and pure guesswork. Much use is made by us all of trial and error – using the clues on the page to produce an idea of what a sentence 'says' and then doing a quick mental check to test whether the interpretation of the words makes sense. If not, we try an alternative version. Normally, all this happens rapidly and we usually get it right first attempt (or skim over the trickier bits!). Listening to a struggling child read, however, you can hear the various versions being hopefully tested out – often with the child concentrating so hard on getting the words off the page that he loses the sense (and certainly the enjoyment) of the story anyway.

This process of cracking the printed code relies on many mental skills, and problems in these are often found in children with reading difficulties. Skill problems that researchers have found in some children with reading difficulties include: difficulty in noticing small differences between similar shapes (like letters), problems in remembering sequences of shapes or sounds, unusual movements of the eyes while reading, poor co-ordination of the body generally, and problems in remembering and recognizing links between shapes and sounds. The problem with all of this is that no one can be certain whether such 'skill problems' cause reading difficulty itself, or the other way round.

Dyslexia

Children with a specific reading difficulty (that is, a serious problem with reading in spite of good general ability in other school work) are sometimes described as being dyslexic. There are many different views about dyslexia and this has unfortunately caused much heated argument. A number of the key points for a parent or teacher concerned about reading problems can be set out as follows:

(i) One in twenty-five British schoolchildren by the age of 9 or 10 has a specific reading difficulty that is nothing to do with his general intelligence.

(ii) In a significant proportion of these children there are also mental skill problems such as those listed above, which may be causes or effects of reading problems.

(iii) It is not clear what causes specific reading difficulty, and it may be caused by many factors rather than only one.

(iv) Dyslexia is a useful term if those using it (a) see it as a 'label' for a reading problem that occurs in an otherwise able child *but* (b) also accept that there are many possible causes for this, and do not see dyslexia as a disease with a single cause to be cured – like mumps.

(v) Children whose main problem is with reading (rather than other school work) are especially unlikely to improve their reading without extra help.

(vi) Paired reading has not been found less suitable for dyslexic children than for those whose reading problem is part of general problems with school work.

Paired reading can equally well be used to help the bright child whose only real problem is with reading, and the child who is finding all his school work difficult. One of the first children with whom paired reading was used had been diagnosed as dyslexic. He was a very bright boy, who seemed able to learn everything except how to read well, and his reading improved with paired reading. At that stage he said to me: 'I know I can read better now, but have I still got dyslexia?' He thought of dyslexia as a disease he had either got or not got – like mumps. The point should have been that he was a person who found reading difficult but that with help he was learning the task better.

Reading and Antisocial Behaviour
There is evidence that reading problems and antisocial behaviour go together in some children. It is possible that some children who read badly not only start failing in their other school work because of this, but also go on to rebel against school and all it stands for. It would be tremendous if, for some children at least, this vicious circle could be stopped by getting them 'hooked' on reading again.

Mistakes in Reading
One of the most frequent comments made by parents of children struggling with their reading is, 'He is so careless – he gets the big, difficult words right but keeps making silly mistakes on all the little ones.' Certainly, the poor reader gets stuck on difficult words,

but many do seem to make things worse by making mistakes on simple words they 'should' be able to manage – like 'if', 'to', 'and'. It is important to know that this is extremely common, and not a sign that your child is particularly careless or lazy. There are three likely reasons for this. Firstly, big words are not actually more difficult to remember once they've been seen once, than the common little words. 'Aeroplane' is not much like other words and is fairly easy to recognize (or to guess correctly when you come across a long word starting with 'ae' in a book with aeroplanes in it!) – but telling the difference between 'if' and 'of' does need closer inspection. Secondly, when a difficult word is spotted coming up in a sentence, there is a natural tendency to look ahead to it and pay less attention to the smaller words leading up to it – increasing the risk of 'careless' mistakes. This is like a mountaineer setting his eyes on the mountain ahead and tripping over a molehill on the way. Thirdly, getting the small 'linking words' in a sentence right (like 'to', 'and', 'so') relies very much on knowing the meaning of the whole sentence. If you are a child spending so much time on fighting with each word that you've lost the meaning of the sentence, then you've also lost your major clue to the smaller words in it.

As an illustration of how the child's reading can suffer if he hasn't grasped the meaning of the sentence as a whole, consider the following sentence with a word missing. 'His mother put his dinner down – the kitchen table.' Knowing the meaning of the sentence, you know that the missing word must be 'on'. But a child who has spent perhaps half a minute struggling to get to that point in the sentence after getting stuck on 'mother' and 'dinner' (and noticing 'kitchen' coming up as the next unknown) quite literally won't have a clue on what should go in the gap. If the word 'on' is there instead of a gap, he may well confuse it with 'no' if he finds the order of letters difficult, because he doesn't have the meaning at his fingertips to guide him as you do. This is like the learner driver who spends so much concentration on making the car go along that he has no idea where he is in town.

Another common feature of children's mistakes is that they manage a word in one place but fail completely with it a few sentences on. Again, as with the learner driver, a skill which has only been half-mastered will work one time but not the next – managing a word (or changing gear smoothly) on one occasion is no guarantee that the success can be repeated next time. Consistently getting it right only comes with practice. It must also be remembered that the same word can actually be harder to read on one page than it is on another, if there are more clues to help on one page than another. The word 'queue' is easier to read in the sentence, 'The people waiting for the bus lined up to form a queue at the bus-stop,' than it is in the sentence, 'The British like to queue.'

Given all these problem areas, reading well seems fraught with difficulties. There are certainly many possible pitfalls – but also, there are plenty of clues to help the child read his way through any written material. Although it is natural to ask why one's own child has problems with reading, and there are many theories on the subject, most answers to this particular question are likely to be as much guesswork as anything else. Rather than hunt a cause for his problems (when there may be many), a better first step in helping a child progress in reading is to work with him on a generally useful technique such as paired reading. If this fails, or if there is some obvious major problem (like poor eyesight), then seek more specialist assessment and help through the back up services (such as educational psychology and specialized remedial services) available to the school.

It is worth offering a helping hand with reading to any child or young adult who is finding it hard going, regardless of the actual gap between his reading and chronological ages.

HELPING WITH READING AT HOME

Before describing paired reading in the next chapter, it is worth looking at the type of help parents can give to the very young child before starting on reading itself, and also at the usual role of parents in hearing their children read.

Getting Used to Books

Before a young child starts leaning what words say and mean, it is helpful for him to become used to books, and interested in them. To set the scene, it is valuable if the child can recognize writing and printing, and know that they contain information or enjoyment he wants.

The best first step in this is to read to the child. Read stories, certainly, but other written things like labels and signs as well. This introduction can be built upon by occasionally pointing to the words as they are read, and showing the child how to turn pages. The idea that the words (rather than the pictures) are where the story comes from, the fact that they are read from left to right and top to bottom, and the mechanics of starting at the front, the right way up, and reading each page until the end, are all useful to master before starting reading itself. Parents can readily make these basic reading skills familiar to the very young child. 'Pre-reading exercises' should however not be overdone or made too complicated. It is important not to put the child off reading, but to get him hooked – to get across the idea that reading is something that might be worth doing.

Hearing the Child Read

The most common existing way in which adults help children read is by 'hearing' them read. This is done with both young beginning readers and older children with reading difficulties. Hearing reading is what most adults (including parents and teachers) will naturally do to help when no more specific instructions have been given.

Someone watching an adult hearing a child read would observe the child reading to a mainly silent adult. The child will occasionally stumble over a word, and from time to time he will get a word wrong, or get completely stuck and stop altogether. When the child gets a word wrong, the adult says 'no', and then supplies the word, or says something like: 'No . . . sound it out.' When the child is stuck altogether, the adult may again say 'sound it out', or something like 'come on, you should know what that is', or 'you got that on the last page, what is it?' (although whatever the child may have got on the last page, he clearly hasn't got it on this one). After a further struggle, if the child hasn't succeeded, the adult will supply the correct word.

If this sounds familiar, consider what is happening from the child's point of view. Firstly, he is working at a task (reading) which is difficult for him, either because he is still learning how to cope with the more difficult words, or because he is already someone who finds reading fluently and correctly a problem. Yet he is succeeding in reading at least some words perfectly correctly. While he is succeeding, however, most of his successful efforts are met with adult silence and, apparently, indifference.

Try an experiment. Without warning them first, ask someone to explain or describe something or some event to you, and while they are doing it you make no positive reactions at all – no nods, 'I see', 'uh-huhs' or smiles. After a short time, you will find such reaction hard to suppress (a bit like those advertisements that challenge you not to chew a particular kind of sweet). You will also probably feel that you are being quite hostile and discouraging, and the other person will eventually be affected by your non-responsiveness. This is precisely what many adults do to children when silently 'hearing them read'.

Watch another adult hearing a child read, and note the number of positive reactions (nods, 'uh-huh's, 'yesscs' etc) that they make. A few people will react positively and frequently, but the vast majority, in the absence of any instructions to the contrary, will give very few positive reactions to the child's correct reading – or none at all. Most adults will give frequent positive reactions to being spoken to, but very few to being read to. While reading, and getting the words right, many children are thus getting no encouragement or positive feedback from the adult. Yet positive reactions from other people or just plain, timely praise for success, has long been recognized as a powerful strengthener of learning and success.

In addition to successful reading being met by silence, many children find practising reading to an adult to be less than pleasant; something to avoid if at all possible. To be told to keep trying when you are stuck on a word can be quite stressful pressure – and enjoyment of whatever book is being read is spoilt by frequent stoppages and failures.

To add to all this, the child who is finding reading difficult is likely to be given simple books to read; books that he knows are meant for younger children. Stories like 'This is the dog. The dog plays ball', rather lose their appeal by the age of 9 or 10. Children still struggling on such books are all too sharply aware that others of the same age are reading well on much more advanced books. A child with reading problems usually has to read 'baby books' when his appetite is for what the good readers of his age and in his class are reading – material that is literally a 'closed book' to him. It must be rather like sitting a 10 year old next to a classmate eating fish and chips, and giving him a tin of babyfood for himself.

Hearing a child read is far better than not helping him at all, despite these drawbacks. Practice at reading at home, with a parent hearing the child sympathetically, does encourage the development of reading skills. It does however have the risks of too much pressure on the child, too much concentration on failures rather than successes in getting words right, lack of praise, and loss of interest if the reading material is too simple and uninteresting. One can, and should, improve on simple 'hearing' in the standard way, in order to increase the interest and benefit of reading practice for the child. The single best improvement one can make is to praise or tell the child when he is reading words correctly. The best improvement beyond this is to use a paired reading approach.

The Parents' Role in Reading

Until relatively recently, reading was seen as the preserve of teachers, and parents were specifically told not to try their own hand at reading work at home in case they simply confused the child and made the teacher's job more difficult. Parents were not normally involved in their children's schooling – in the early 1970's the school around the corner from where I lived bore the notice by the doorway 'No parents beyond this point'. Textbooks on reading made no reference at all to parents being encouraged to help teach reading, either to beginners or to older children with difficulties. Where reading problems existed, the advice in the textbooks was that only a highly specialized remedial programme, tailor-made for each individual child by experts, would achieve results. There was no acceptance that time spent on reading by parent and child would help.

Much has now changed. Most schools encourage parents to help their children at home and to become involved at school in a variety of ways. Reading is, increasingly, something parents and teachers co-operate over. (Before parents often did help at home – but didn't tell teachers because they were known to disapprove!) Many schools have formal home/school reading schemes of one type or another.

A major step in accepting that parents should be involved in their children's reading came with an experiment in Haringey, London, in which parents helping with reading at home was found to improve children's reading. At first, a study of the *differences* in children's reading skills noted that a key factor in better readers was that their parents regularly heard them read at home. In the experiment which followed, parents in some top infants' classes were asked to hear their children read, and the progress of these children was compared with children whose parents were not doing this. Not only did those with parents helping do significantly better, but they kept up their improvement over two years.

The importance of the Haringey project is that it showed that parents can help their children's reading with good results. Since that project other studies (particularly those on paired reading), have shown that by using straightforward but specific reading techniques, parents can produce very impressive improvements in their children's reading. Some of the most effective home/school reading schemes now use paired reading as their key method.

Apart from the acceptance that parents can and should help their children read, another recent development is the use of parents as remedial helpers of their children. The longstanding advice of the textbooks that only tailor-made expert remedial teaching will help the struggling reader has now given way to the view that parents can help the struggling reader at home. Depending on how severe his problems are, the child may need remedial specialist and parents working in partnership.

The best advice to parents at present is – firstly, try to keep your child interested in things written; secondly encourage his progress from first words to highly developed skill by using paired reading or a related technique at home; thirdly, if your child finds reading hard try regular paired reading and monitor its effects in conjunction with the school, but if that fails to produce results, then seek more specialized help.

TWO: INTRODUCTION TO PAIRED READING

The aim of this chapter is to describe paired reading, and then to set out its main characteristics as a means of helping children read. To give a clear description of the technique, paired reading will be described as someone watching it being done would see it, without at this stage going into the reasoning behind what is being done. The theory behind each step, and tips on how to do it and how to avoid problems will follow in later chapters.

A Description of Paired Reading

Someone watching a parent and child doing paired reading would see firstly a book being chosen to use in paired reading sessions, and then the parent and child sitting together for these sessions regularly (probably once each day, for about a quarter of an hour each session) at home. I am assuming that the parent and child have already learned together how to do paired reading. I usually teach each parent and child 'pair' on their own, which normally takes about one to one and a half hours. Some people train parents in groups and those learning directly from this handbook should expect to practise for one to one and a half hours before mastering the technique.

In choosing a book, the child is asked to pick *any* book he really wants to read, regardless of whether it is difficult for him (he is going to get the help he needs, when he needs it, to enable him to manage a difficult book). The ideal is a book suitable for children of his actual (chronological) age rather than his reading age. To be avoided is anything too young for him, but which may get chosen because of his reading problems. A book may be chosen from those already at home, at school, in a bookshop, or from the public library. The final choice of book is the child's – it is what *he* wants to read, not what an adult thinks he ought to read! While what is chosen is usually a book, a comic or even a set of instructions (e.g. for a game or making a model) will do. Special books for paired reading are *not* needed.

Once the book is chosen, the observer will see parent (usually Mum!) and child sit side-by-side with the book placed so that they can both see it. They may be at a table, or on the settee or the edge of a bed. They will do their best to go somewhere quiet – away from T.V., dog, brothers and sisters.

Parent and child will now begin reading from the book, out loud and together. They will say each word at the same time as one another – rather like reading a duet. The observer may notice that they are reading at a steady rhythm to keep themselves saying each word together and that Mum is using her finger to keep pace by pointing to each word as they begin to say it. Our observer will also perhaps be surprised at the difficult words the child is managing to read alongside his mother – words he would be unlikely to manage on his own.

Whenever parent and child don't manage to read a word together – perhaps the child doesn't manage the word, or one of the pair begins to read on ahead of the other – the mother points to the problem word and they try it again together.

This is 'reading together', the first of the two halves of paired reading. The other half is 'reading alone', and the changeover from 'together' to 'alone' reading happens whenever the child wants it to. At some point while parent and child are reading together, the child will knock on the table or some other convenient surface. This is his signal that he wants to try reading alone for a bit.

As soon as the child signals, the parent stops reading aloud, and the child carries on reading aloud on his own. While the child is getting words right – whether he manages only one word alone, complete sentences or even whole pages – his mother will keep saying 'yes', 'right', 'correct', 'good', 'well done', 'uh-huh' or whatever else is natural to both of them, to let him know that he is reading correctly. Quite unlike the silence with which most adults hear a child reading correctly, there is a constant feedback of praise from parent to child. Particular praise will be given for reading a word that has caused problems in the past.

Before long, the child will hit a problem. He will get stuck on his own, he will read a word wrongly, or perhaps miss a word out. When this happens, his Mother will point to the problem word if he hasn't noticed his mistake, but will only leave him trying to get the word for about four seconds. There is no prompting or instruction to 'sound it out' – simply praise if the child begins to get it right. At the end of about four seconds, the parent points to the word and the parent and child read the word aloud together. Then the pair carry on reading aloud together (in exactly the same way as they began the session) until the child again 'knocks' as his signal to try reading alone again. Our observer may be interested to note that the child can manage to read the word he was stuck on, correctly first time, now that he is doing it with his parent. He does not need to be told what it is first, before the two of them can read it aloud together.

If the child is finding the book fairly easy, he will knock again very soon to carry on alone, possibly after just one word read together. If he is new to paired reading, or the book is quite hard, he may wait for an easy few words to come up, perhaps a few paragraphs later, before knocking again.

To recap; the parent and child sit side-by-side where they can both see the book – which is one the child very much wants to read but may find quite difficult because it is suitable for his actual age rather than his reading age. They both read aloud together, saying each word in unison, with Mum keeping the pace by pointing to each word; and pointing a second time to any word they need to try again. When the child wants to try reading alone, he 'knocks' and Mum stops. He carries on alone – Mum praising him for what he gets right. Mum points out mistakes with her finger, and starts reading aloud together with him again every time he is stuck or can't put a mistake right within about four seconds. They carry on together until he knocks again.

It is rather like a car with two gears – 'together' gear and 'alone' gear. You always start off in 'together' gear and the child always controls the changeover to 'alone' gear by knocking to make the change. The parent controls the change back to 'together' gear by joining in again whenever the child is stuck for four seconds.

Our observer will have noted a number of special features that make paired reading 'different'. These are: (i) the stress on the child choosing his own book, (ii) the time spent reading together, which adults don't normally do with children, (iii) the praise, or 'feedback' to the child while he is getting words right on his own, (iv) the fact that the child rather than the adult decides when he can do without the adult's help for a bit, and (v) that the child is never left struggling with a word, or pressed to 'keep on trying' – four seconds is the longest he is left before help comes. What will also be apparent is that the child usually enjoys doing paired reading, and that both parent and child have a clear pattern of what to do.

FEATURES OF PAIRED READING

Simplicity
Paired reading is not in any way mysterious or particularly complicated. What has just been described can be mastered by most people with a little practice. It does need the tutor to be able to read better than the child who is being helped – but it has been used successfully by parents who have some difficulty with reading themselves. It is also increasingly used in schools with an older child (or sometimes even a good reader of the same age) helping a younger child or poorer reader.

Because paired reading is simple, you do not have to be a specialist, or experienced, or to attend special courses to be able to do it. While it is easier if you can watch someone else doing it at first, many teachers and psychologists have begun paired reading, very effectively, by reading about it rather than seeing it done. There is no reason why many parents and many more teachers should not do the same. I would comment that it is better to follow written instructions than to learn by watching someone who may be doing things wrongly! One mother I worked with a few weeks ago had 'picked up' paired reading by watching a poor example by another mother, and had completely missed out the giving of praise, but added demands to her son to 'sound it out' instead of helping him after about four seconds. Since research has found paired reading to be effective as a whole 'package', changing it as drastically as this may well drastically change its effects.

The two main advantages of paired reading being simple are that it is easily mastered in a short time and that it is readily used at home. Most households with children have meals to cook, little ones to feed, ironing to do, T.V. to watch, lost shoes to find, and collections of objects to be assembled and taken to Cubs or Brownies in an hour's time, all at the same time as coping with reading help. Paired reading does appear simple enough to remain a practical proposition in most normal homes!

Flexibility
I originally designed paired reading as a remedial reading technique for Junior-age school children, but it has proved suitable for very much younger children (down to those first learning to read), older children, teenagers, and even adults. It has also been found suitable for children and young people with widely differing reading abilities (including, recently, helping those with normal reading skills to progress further). As it was designed to do, it also copes with the range of

books or other reading material from the very simple to the extremely complicated. It has been effectively used with handicapped children.

The flexibility of paired reading has become one of its strongest features. The flexibility comes from the fact that the technique automatically provides the child with help whenever it is needed (when a problem cannot be overcome with only four seconds of effort) and keeps the help going as long as it is needed (until the child 'knocks' to try alone again). If the rules are followed, therefore, the amount of help given is automatically linked to how much help is needed. A child with very poor reading skills or a very difficult book will simply, and quite automatically, produce more 'reading together' and much shorter spells of 'reading alone', while on the other hand, the better reader or simpler book will produce less 'reading together' and more 'reading alone'. Although paired reading will sound different to an observer when different levels of reading ability or books of different levels of difficulty are involved, the paired reading technique itself is exactly the same. Just by following the basic rules, one can use paired reading regardless of the degree of reading difficulty your pupil or child has, with whatever book he or she chooses to read.

Enjoyment
Most children and parents find paired reading enjoyable to do. The children with whom I have worked on paired reading schemes, and most of their parents, have reported that paired reading was definitely better than they had expected extra reading would be. An enjoyable technique has three distinct advantages: it increases the child's motivation and interest in working on reading; parents and children are more likely to be able to keep it going over a reasonable period at home; it can sometimes be used with a child who has become 'anti' the whole idea of reading.

There are probably a number of reasons why paired reading is enjoyed by most people. Firstly, the routines of trying to read together, and of the child 'knocking', can become almost a game rather than something too serious. Secondly, the less enjoyable aspects of 'extra reading' have been left out – no excessive pressures and no long periods of struggling and failing to get words. Thirdly, the parent giving praise is itself a positive step towards enjoying the session. Finally, and for the child probably most important of all, paired reading allows him to read 'real' books that he really wants to read – not special books or books that are too young for him. It may be the first time that he has been able to tackle something he genuinely wants to read or that his friends are reading, and for many children paired reading gives them their first free access to the world of books. Because the paired reading rules give the child help when he needs it, and do not break up everything he tries to read with long struggles and hold-ups while he is stuck, the technique enables him to progress through his book. Therefore he can actually follow and enjoy the story, rather than spending all his efforts on the struggle to read.

Parent-Child Relationship
Paired reading was never designed to help cement good relationships between parent and child, but many who have published reports on its effects have commented that it appears to do just this. Certainly, parent and child working together on something which is usually enjoyable and which normally produces results, can help to develop a friendly working relationship. It is also important that instead of the child being the fail-ure and the parent getting frustrated from time to time, paired reading puts parent and child on an unusually equal footing. The child is no longer constantly failing while the parent asks him to 'try again' and the parent has a clear set of rules to follow – which the child may need to remind her of! Many parents and children have 'fallen out' to some extent over past efforts to hear the struggling reader read, and paired reading can often make working together on reading pleasant again for

both. Working successfully on a problem together, with a set of clear rules to avoid arguments, does seem to bring many mothers and children pleasantly close.

Paired Reading used with other Approaches

It was noted in Chapter One that paired reading does not conflict with other approaches to reading. This is perhaps one of its most important features. The last thing one wants to do is to confuse the child by asking him to work out words differently at home and at school, or differently with different teachers.

Paired reading does not confuse the child because it does not ask him to work out words in any particular way, nor does it ask him to stop using any methods of working out words that he has already been taught or has invented for himself. It simply gives help when needed, help by giving the right words by example rather than by using any particular method of working them out, together with praise to encourage success. Paired reading encourages success — however the child achieves it.

Because of this lack of conflict with other approaches to reading, a parent may use paired reading at home with no fear of damaging what is going on at school, and a teacher may use it *as well as* any other method of remedial reading he or she may be using. Paired reading is therefore something of a 'universal booster' to any child's reading.

Common Sense

A compliment that has been paid to paired reading is the comment that 'there's nothing new in it, most of it's as old as the hills.' Certainly there is nothing at all novel about praise, about helping by example, or even about reading together. What produces results is this particular combination of common sense elements — and moreover, this particular combination used consistently, regularly, and over a period of time. The principles and pieces of paired reading are not new, but putting them together this way is. What matters is that the combination seems to work, that it is not the usual way of helping children read – so it is worth trying – and that its ingredients are well-tried and tested.

Economics

Paired reading is a cheap technique to use, and it is 'cost effective' in that it seems to give children a good amount of help for very little expenditure. For a parent, the time spent is the only cost; there is no need to buy any special materials or books. For the school, setting up a paired reading scheme with parents involves relatively little staff time to train and support the parents concerned. A successful scheme produces far more direct reading training for each child at home than could possibly be managed in the classroom. Far more children can be helped this way at home, with good effect, than could be helped at school by remedial teachers or remedial units. In these days of limited resources in education, any technique with relatively little demand for finance or staff time deserves consideration. The one caution I would give is that in order to produce results and maintain consistency in the use of the technique, it is important for any school undertaking a paired reading scheme to plan for the continuing supervision and support for parents. It is false economy to give good initial training but to fail to provide enough follow-up.

Local education authorities are these days constantly asked to work to 'the three E's' of Economy, Efficiency and Effectiveness. Paired reading schemes would seem to be well in line with these requirements.

Research

Paired reading has been studied, researched and evaluated by many psychologists, teachers and other educators, in this country and abroad. It is probably the most widely evaluated technique in education.

The overall findings of this research into paired reading are summarised in Chapter Eight. Here, though, I wish to make one comment about using a technique with many positive research results behind it. This is that it is important to use paired reading as it was designed – because this is what has been found to produce the positive results. There are some variations which have been the subject of research studies – but unless one is varying the technique in order to evaluate the variation systematically, and in a properly designed research study, changes from 'standard' paired reading carry the risk of not producing the usual positive results. Avoid the temptation to try to 'improve' on paired reading, or to leave bits out of it, unless you are researching variations. Stick to the tried and tested formula.

... And Some Negatives

This chapter has concentrated upon the positive features of paired reading. Nothing, however, escapes some disadvantages, and paired reading does have some.

For the parent, to do paired reading does demand a continuing and regular commitment of time at home, and sometimes this can be difficult to achieve. This may be the case at half-term or holiday times, when paired reading needs to continue but parent and child's time together is interrupted by camps, school trips, stays with grandparents, and other children coming to stay. For some families, a regular daily session is difficult – as, for instance, in the large single-parent family.

A second potential problem is that because paired reading is a skill the parent has to learn, the child does need to work with a parent (or other person) who has taken the trouble to learn properly how to do it. A Mum who is expert at paired reading can, with care, train Dad, or someone else in the family, to do it as well – but no-one else could ever just 'step in' to help the child if a person who has learned paired reading is not around. When paired reading is 'picked up' and tried by someone else in the family without them following the original instructions or being taught how to do it, I find the results decidedly odd, and often nothing like paired reading is supposed to be. This does run the risk of confusing the child. (I even came across one boy recently who said 'Mum couldn't read with me last week, so I did paired reading on my own.' I wish now that I had asked him to demonstrate this feat!)

For the school organizing a paired reading scheme, it has already been noted that one cannot cut the costs of proper initial training of parents (or other tutors) *and* of regular follow-up support and supervision. There is therefore a sustained commitment of resources, albeit modest.

Paired reading remains the most commonly used and widely suitable of the various special ways for parents to help children at home. It must however be noted that some educators have found the need to develop special variations of paired reading for two special groups of children – the very youngest children starting to learn to read for the first time, and children whose reading has already progressed well and who may benefit from a more advanced form of paired reading after successfully using the standard technique described at the start of this chapter. These special versions, and their uses, are described in Chapter Seven.

The advantages of paired reading *not* insisting on the child working words out in a particular manner have already been set out. There is however one disadvantage to this – paired reading does not single out words the child has particular difficulty with to give him special guidance in coping with these. There are techniques for parents to use that add this factor (again, they are referred to in Chapter Seven) – *but* they cannot be used as widely as paired reading. The price they pay for being more complicated than paired reading is that they need parents to be more specially trained, and special materials may be needed, rather than using *any* written material as in paired reading. They also have yet to be found as generally usable and effective as paired reading.

It is important to stress again that the teacher or

parent should not try to graft onto paired reading any particular method of working words out. That could lose all the advantages of paired reading. Unless one is an educational researcher, stick with the point that paired reading as described in this handbook is safe for general use.

THREE: HOW PAIRED READING WORKS

Having described paired reading in the last chapter, and run through its key features, my intention in this chapter is to give a brief explanation of the theory behind why it works.

I originally designed paired reading using 'behavioural' principles – that is, principles concerned with how we *learn* to change our behaviour or build up skills, according to a number of basic 'rules'. These are the principles I have mainly used below in describing the theory behind each bit of paired reading. A number of paired reading researchers have put forward other possible explanations for how paired reading works. It is more than likely that, given how complicated a skill reading is, a whole range of different principles are at work in paired reading, as well as the basic 'behavioural' ones that it was originally based on. I have added some of the most important of these below – but there are probably other 'ingredients' to be found in the future as well.

Reading Together
One of the most important ways in which we all learn to do things is by example – by following someone else's 'model' of what we are learning to do. This kind of learning is most powerful when we are trying our own hand at a task at the same time as someone is showing us what to do.

In the 'reading together' part of paired reading, the tutor is giving the child a constant example to follow of how the words should sound, at exactly the same time as the child is trying them for himself. This 'joining in with the example' makes use of a very powerful form of learning. The child is helped by having both the printed words and his parent's voice to follow in his attempts to read the words. He also has a model of correct reading constantly there as a check on whether he is reading the words correctly or not. He is thus aware of exactly how he is doing all the time, and can use this 'feedback' to tell him how to adjust his own reading to get it right – even in the middle of a word. This is much more efficient in helping him get words right than simply telling him he's wrong when he's already finished a word, and then telling him to 'sound it out'.

Reading together does *teach* the child how to read, because he is constantly correcting his own reading to fit his parent's model. It is not just telling him the answers. The only way he can keep reading the words at the same time as Mum is by keeping up, adjusting and improving his own efforts.

It is remarkable how in reading together, a child can often manage a word he does not know at all, first time with Mum. I find it helpful to explain to the child that Mum is giving him a 'piggy-back' through the tricky word, and as long as he keeps going with her, rather than stopping or waiting for her, they will both end up on the other side of the word with it safely read between them. A word read a few times this way is usually learned and remembered.

In short, the main principle behind reading together is that the child learns by constantly adjusting his version of the words on the page, to the model of correct reading supplied for him by his parent. As well as this, it is likely that his motivation to get words right – and his understanding of what he is reading – is increased because he is getting through his story at a reasonable, instead of painfully slow, speed. He is also likely to pick up alongside his parent some of the clues she is using to suggest the correct reading of particular words, because he is concentrating on the same things she is, but with the benefit of her example.

Reading Alone with Praise

In the 'reading alone' part of paired reading, the child gains practice in getting right most of the words he has learned from Mum's example while reading together. This practice helps him to remember these words, because he is not only repeating them and therefore becoming more familiar with them, but Mum's praise for getting them right leaves him in no doubt that he has read them properly. This 'seals them in' to his mind.

One of the most basic principles in learning anything is that when something we do is followed by something pleasant, the action or skill involved is strengthened for the future. This is the principle of 'reinforcement' – pleasant consequences strengthen any action or skill, and make us more likely to repeat it. This has been shown by a massive amount of research to be one of the basic building blocks of learning any skill, and it applies to skills as varied as flying an aeroplane, learning to feed oneself, playing darts – and reading. The praise tutors are asked to give children in the reading alone part of paired reading is quite specifically there to 'seal in' and reinforce each bit of successful reading the child does.

As we noted in Chapter One, it is amazing and sad that even though we respond positively to a child speaking to us, we do not usually give any responses at all to him when he is reading, correctly, to us. Despite all the evidence that praise is likely to strengthen his skill, at reading as at anything else, we constantly miss the opportunity to 'seal in' any of his successful efforts at reading during the traditional 'listening to him read'. I ask parents and children, when I see them about reading for the first time, to show me what they do together (if anything) to help with reading at home, and I count the number of positive reactions the child is given for words read correctly. While there are exceptions, the vast majority of parents who have not been advised on this point, react positively to no more than one or two words in a hundred. This is nowhere near enough; the child needs a constant patter of positive reaction while he is succeeding so that he is never left in any doubt as to whether what he has read is correct or not.

The praise during reading alone serves two distinct purposes. Firstly, it strengthens the child's reading skills (i.e. whatever method he is using to get the words right) – as any positive response will do. Secondly, it serves as a 'feedback' to him that he is still reading correctly. If you listen carefully to a child reading a difficult book aloud, you will notice that he reads some words in an unsure, questioning voice, because he is not sure whether what he has said is correct. (He may occasionally not only read the word as if it had a question mark after it, but may even look up at you for a reassurance that he is right.) If you fail to respond, he has not learned the word, even if it was correct – because he doesn't *know* it was. If you confirm that he's right, on other words as well as those he questions like this, he is learning. Equally, praising what is correct but pointing out mistakes as the paired reading rules require, prevents him learning mistakes as he reads.

When the child is reading very slowly, managing only a few words each time he reads alone, he will be getting praise for most of the words he reads. As he speeds up, but the tutor keeps the same 'patter' going, he will naturally begin reading many more words for each word of praise. The parent or other tutor will also single out for special praise words he has got right for the first time, particularly difficult words, and occasions when he manages to correct a mistake for himself. This is valuable in teaching him to read, because praise for these events 'seals in' important steps of progress for the child.

I have said a lot about 'praise' but there are two common objections to using praise like this that must be considered. Firstly, that praise may sound silly – particularly to the teenager. My comment on this is that the praise has to fit the child; a five year old may respond well to 'good', 'smashing', 'clever boy' and cuddles (these count as positive responses too) – but a six foot seventeen year old won't thank you for that choice of praise! Teenagers do however welcome responses like 'yes', 'mmh-hmm' and 'right'. If in doubt, during a conversation note what you say when responding positively to the person concerned. Adults also are helped in learning by adult-appropriate praise – in teaching an adult to drive I will reinforce correct manœuvres by adult-appropriate comments like 'yes', 'that's it' or even 'well done'. No one is too old to be helped by appropriate praise.

The parent or teacher who makes a wrong choice of praise at times may be reassured by my experience in the earliest days of paired reading. One of the first children I tried it with was in the 'reading alone' phase for the first time, and I was sitting next to him saying 'good boy'. He stopped reading, glared at me, and said 'I wish you'd stop saying that – I'm not a dog!' While I sat in worried silence at this body-blow to my theories, he carried on reading aloud. A few lines further on, he stopped again and said: 'Could you tell me when I'm correct though?' So I switched my praise to 'correct' and we carried on famously!

The second objection often made to using praise in paired reading is that it might distract the child. If the right kind of praise for the child is being used, very few children do in practice find it distracting. Most, if asked, will say that they find being told they are getting words right a help rather than a hindrance. At first, the very unfamiliarity of praise while reading will feel 'odd'; but it rapidly becomes familiar. Praise is probably far less distracting than being left unsure of some words.

The strong effect of praise in paired reading has been demonstrated when some children were asked to change their normal paired reading technique. These children had been praised for knocking on the table to signal the change to reading alone, and had learned to signal very soon after they had been helped with a mistake. When asked *not* to signal so quickly (when new tutors were being shown the techniques) they found they could not stop themselves. Having been praised for signalling quickly after mistakes they had learned the action too efficiently to stop it.

During paired reading, praise is an added ingredient to reading sessions. Once the child's reading improves enough for him to read more for himself, outside paired reading sessions, other forms of positive consequences for reading correctly begin to come into play. One of these is the positive experience of managing to read a book, comic or something else that used to be too difficult. Demonstrating to oneself that one is improving is as good as – or better than – praise in reinforcing the skill, and success does tend to breed success. Beyond this, reading successfully enough to go at a reasonable speed through a book, and to get enough words right to understand the text properly, means that reading starts being reinforced by its own reward – that of enjoying the book.

Signalling

The thinking behind the child signalling when he wants to read alone is that the child is always in control of his parent's help. The help doesn't stop until *he* feels ready to let go of it. Because of this, the child only reads alone when he feels confident enough to try – which should reduce to a minimum any risk of being left to struggle on his own.

There is a built-in tendency for the child to signal (rather than stay always in the reading together phase) as he becomes used to paired reading, for a number of reasons. He is praised for each signal; he receives praise while he is correctly reading alone; and he can usually read ahead faster and thus enjoy the book more when reading alone than when reading together. When paired reading is first started, the child will naturally signal very little and will need to be prompted (prompted, not pressed, by suggestions that he try a signal rather than demands that he does. As he becomes more confident, he will eventually try.) As he progresses, he will signal more often and the proportion of time spent reading alone rather than reading together will go up. This is a sign of improvement in both reading skill and confidence.

Rapid Help with Problems

In giving the child help after only four seconds of being stuck on a problem word (by reverting to reading together) the parent is keeping the pressure and stress out of reading. The stress of the more traditional 'try it again' approach is reversed, and reading becomes more attractive to the child as a result.

The four second limit before help is given also ensures that the child can enjoy progressing through his book, concentrating on the story rather than losing it in his struggles to work words out.

Reducing the stress on the child by reading a problem word together after four seconds does *not* simply give the child an easy time by letting him off the hook and not making him try hard enough. Reading the word with him after four seconds is more in line with the principles of efficient learning than asking him to keep trying unsuccessfully. Too much pressure or stress interferes with learning rather than encouraging it: we learn best when we are motivated but not pressured to learn. The thinking behind the rapid help given in paired reading is: a) after about four seconds of effort, it is likely that continued struggling will produce enough frustration and stress to *reduce* the chances of getting the word right and learning it; b) if the child hasn't managed it in four seconds the chances of working it out are low anyway; c) reading the problem word together is an effective way of teaching the word – by the child adjusting his efforts to Mum's example; d) the motivation to remember the word after reading it together is there, because getting it right while reading alone later on results in praise.

The way help is given in paired reading is intended to reduce the mistakes made by the child (they are always corrected, and he is not asked to keep guessing at a word). The emphasis is on getting words right rather than concentrating on errors and how to correct them. While it is true that this may not give some children instruction in avoiding their particular type of mistake, for most children the learning principle of producing and then practising and reinforcing correct results is a sound one. Additionally, the child's interest in reading and desire to read, often much battered by failure in reading, are vital and more likely to be increased by concentrating on what he can read than on what he can't.

Free Choice of Book

The thinking behind giving the child a free choice of reading material, allowing him to choose something he really wants to read even if it is too difficult for him to read on his own, has already been discussed. To sum it up: the child is not put off by having to use an 'early' or babyish book; the parent or teacher does not have to buy any special books or materials; the child is motivated to read because *he* wants to; the resulting more positive attitude to reading sessions makes them more likely to happen and makes learning during them more likely to happen as well. Paired reading not only helps the child with his reading, but it also opens up for him the contents of the books his friends are reading. It is also useful that paired reading can be used with anything written or printed, not just books. Because it only needs the child, a tutor, and something (anything) to read, it can be used anywhere – one child and Mother I taught paired reading to told me they had used it to read together the label on a tube of suntan cream on the beach!

An interesting point on the free choice of book to use in paired reading has emerged with some children. This is that the child who has a very unusual taste in books (perhaps wanting to read highly technical books about a special hobby) can still use these in his paired reading sessions. I can think of two particular children who have illustrated the advantages of this; both of them found the books they were offered at school boring. One was a teenage boy whose major hobby was studying World War Two tanks. He chose the most difficult book I have ever used in paired reading – a book of the technical specifications of *German* World

War Two tanks. We used it, his attitude to reading sessions became much more positive, and he learned to read a number of extremely difficult and unusual words. The important thing was that he was learning to cope with the type of reading material that he wanted to use his reading skills for. The other child was a younger boy who had rejected most of the books in various reading schemes – because he wanted to read non-fiction, and simply disliked stories.

When we leave school, we usually choose much of our reading material for ourselves – paired reading lets the child do this even while he is being helped to learn to read. He enjoys it as much as we do.

Conclusion

To sum up, paired reading probably works because of the learning 'rules' it was based on. These are learning words from Mum's example while reading together, practising words during reading alone, having successful reading 'sealed in' and made more likely by praise being given for reading correctly, and learning being encouraged by avoiding stress, failures and mistakes as far as possible, together with a likely positive attitude to the whole thing because the child *wants* to read the book he has chosen.

Added to this, the child can keep up a good 'flow' of reading, at a reasonable speed, during paired reading, and this doubtless involves the child's use of clues from the overall meaning of the sentence to suggest what particular words might be. You can only get the help of such clues if you are reading fairly fast and understanding what the text is all about – as you are doing in paired reading, but are not doing when every word is a struggle and a delay. Being relaxed rather than tense while reading, and enjoying it more than before, is likely to bring out as much success as possible.

It has also been noted that paired reading automatically adjusts itself to different children, different books and different amounts of confidence from one session to the next. The tutor does not have to decide how much help to give. The 'four-second rule' makes sure that help arrives whenever it is needed, however frequently or rarely, and the 'signalling with a knock' rule ensures that help carries on as long as it is wanted. The paired reading rules thus provide the right 'doses of help' for whatever difficulty the child is having with a particular book at a particular time.

While paired reading uses definite rules of how people learn, there are probably many other factors in how it works. It may well work as much by getting rid of previous obstacles to reading (such as stress, failure, boredom, anxiety and uninteresting books), as by introducing anything new. Paired reading perhaps reintroduces reading to the child who has been failing at it, bringing about a more positive interest in reading at the same time as removing obstacles and making success (and praise for it) much more likely. Because it does not make the child use any particular method of working words out, but instead encourages by success and praise anything he tries that actually works, it will automatically strengthen any methods he uses which do work for him, and discourage any which don't.

FOUR: HOW TO DO PAIRED READING

The aim of this chapter is to give a step-by-step guide on how to do paired reading, from scratch. I have written it as guidance to a parent starting paired reading with her own child. It can therefore be read and used directly by such a parent, or by a teacher as the basis for his or her own training of parents. The chapter should also help the parent or teacher who has tried paired reading already, but not succeeded with it so far for lack of clear guidance on how to do it.

The rules for paired reading are listed as a summary for quick reference at the end of the chapter. You may find it easiest to read the relevant section of the chapter before trying each step in practice, and keeping the summary open as a reminder by you when you try the step with the child.

Explaining to the Child

The first step in using paired reading is to explain what is involved to the child and to get him sufficiently interested to agree to try it. The description of paired reading at the start of Chapter Two should help in explaining what it is. Depending on the child's age and understanding, it can be explained that you and he are going to try a way of reading together that has helped many other children to read better, and that most children who have tried it have liked it. He can choose any book he likes, he will be helped with *all* the difficult words, and he will never be made to try too hard if he is stuck. You will read with him to help him through the difficult bits whenever he wants you to, and will do your best to help him enjoy reading his book and to keep going, without making him stop to work things out all the time.

Choosing a Book

There is a great temptation for a parent or teacher to fall into one of two traps when choosing a book for paired reading. Firstly, to try to persuade the child to choose a book that doesn't seem too difficult for him, even if he isn't very keen on it. Secondly, to give him too much guidance – like picking three or four books that you think he *should* like and then pressing him to pick the one he likes best of the few you are offering. The child is not used to having a free choice of what to read, and he needs plenty of time and encouragement to try something he fancies – even if you think it inappropriate or too difficult. The child with reading problems choosing a book is like the adult going into a strange foreign restaurant for the first time – one needs time to work out what to have.

Aim to help the child choose, without over-helping. Spend time with the child going around the bookshelves at home, school library, public library or bookshop. When starting paired reading it is an excellent time to join the library for the first time. Let him use all his tickets and come away with an armful of different books.

Remember that the guideline is to *find a book which the child wants to read, even if it is 'too difficult' for him, which is appropriate for a child of his age.* Avoid books which are too young for him or specially simplified for poor readers. Tips for success are; (a) suggest he chooses a selection of very different books – if he finds one not to his taste he can then switch to something else; (b) let him experiment even with a seemingly 'wild' choice at first (an 11 year old boy I worked with recently had been stuck with readers in class that had no more than four simple words to most sentences – and began paired reading quite successfully with a crime thriller from the library. It was, after all, his first taste of free choice in reading, and he made the most of it!); (c) only 'ban' a book he wants if it is the sort of book you would not let any child of his age read, whether he had reading problems or not, and (d) if a tutor who is going to do paired reading with him is an older child, a better reader of similar age or an adult who finds reading hard, check that the child chooses books the tutor can cope with. Remember that you don't have to use a book – a comic or newspaper will do just as well.

If you are faced with shelves full of books and no ideas on where to start, suggest looking at books to do with any special hobbies or interest the child has, books that go with television programmes he likes, or books he has noticed a friend reading. This is a good time to start 'browsing' in shops or libraries. Encourage him to take books from shelves, thumb through them, put them back if he's not keen, and *enjoy* spending time choosing what to take.

A final point on choice of book: there are no prizes for plodding to the bitter end of a book he thought he'd like, but doesn't. If the child 'goes off' the book during paired reading, tell him he can swop it for another one. He can change books whenever he wants. It is an advantage to have books of different levels of difficulty and different subject matter around when doing paired reading at home, so that the child can swop between easier and harder books, or stick to a single book he finds he likes, as he wishes.

Where to do Paired Reading
Try to choose a place to do paired reading which is comfortable but away from family distractions – especially the other children and the T.V. A table is useful to put the book on, but is not essential. The book can be held on a lap. Tutor and child must however be able to sit side by side. Usual places for paired reading sessions at home are at the kitchen or dining room table, on the settee, or sitting together on the edge of the bed.

Experiment to find out which side of each other you prefer to sit. Few disagree over this (if you do, then follow the child's preference), but trying to do paired reading the 'uncomfortable' way round will not help.

When to do Paired Reading

Set aside a regular time to do paired reading together each day. A little, regularly, is far better than a blitz every now and again. The ideal is to spend a quarter of an hour every day at paired reading. If neither of you wants to stop at the end of a session, you can by all means carry on to about half an hour – but do not go on beyond that. Never keep going beyond quarter of an hour if the child doesn't want to: the price of pushing him to keep going longer is all too often a reluctance to face long sessions again, and a risk of giving up altogether.

Avoid making paired reading sessions a chore that stops the child from doing some favourite activity, or you will put him off it. Do not make him read instead of playing football, watching his favourite T.V. programme, or going to Scouts. A number of girls I have worked with on paired reading recently are keen Guides, and we have gone to great lengths to make sure that sessions of reading fit in around Guide activities.

Two useful tricks in choosing times a child won't mind doing paired reading are to fix the reading session to finish just before a favourite T.V. programme (it helps to follow the session with something rewarding), or to agree that paired reading is done last thing at night with a slightly later bedtime (so that it is something he's allowed to stay up for!).

Deciding who does the Tutoring

As I have already commented, Mum is usually the parent who does the tutoring. This is fine if the family are happy with it – but it is worth discussing which parent should do the job, or whether both should learn how to do it. In some families, one parent is often out in the evenings (it may be Mum or Dad who is out), and other times of the day may not be suitable for paired reading sessions. Where one or both parents have reading difficulties decide which parent is likely to cope best.

The tutor need not always be a parent. Other relatives (such as Grandparents and Aunts) can help, older children can help if they are prepared to learn to do paired reading properly, and suitable volunteers can also help. Volunteers helping at school can do paired reading with children at school, either as well as a parent doing it at home, or instead if there is a problem in doing it at home. In some schools, children of the same age but different reading abilities – carefully chosen to work together – have successfully done paired reading together.

There are three rules to choosing a tutor for any particular child: a) the tutor must be someone acceptable to the child, b) the tutor must be prepared to learn properly how to do paired reading (e.g. by following or being taught the instructions in this chapter), and c) the tutor must be a better reader than the child. It does not matter at all if the tutor has some problems with reading, as long as he or she is good enough to cope with the book and give the child a correct example to follow. It is quite acceptable for a tutor occasionally to tell the child that she doesn't know a word either. I had to admit that sometimes when reading books on specifications of German tanks with the boy I mentioned earlier!

A final comment on choosing tutors is a reminder of what has been said before – someone who has not learned how to do paired reading properly should not step in and try it. If for some reason the usual tutor is not available it is better to miss sessions altogether than to do paired reading with someone who has not learned it properly.

The First Session – Reading Together
Spend the first session, when neither you nor the child have done paired reading before, practising 'reading together'.

Sit next to each other so that you can both see the book clearly – don't make the child peer over to see it, and if you're holding the book on your lap (especially if it is a paperback) make sure the page isn't at such an angle that one of you is trying to read up a slope!

Agree that you, as the tutor, will point to the words as they need to be read, and make it clear that you are both going to try to read each word *at exactly the same time*. Expect the first few efforts at this to be a disaster – they usually are – and have fun together at your first disastrous attempts. Don't take it too seriously. Don't expect to succeed at once (reading together is a skill that has got to be practised – it's not quite as simple as it sounds), and don't blame each other when it goes wrong. Think of it as being like doing a three-legged race together – awkward to do, fun to try, and something which you will shortly get the hang of doing.

As a signal for you both to begin reading together, lift your finger off the page and then put it down under the first word when you are both ready. Make sure the child knows this is his signal. Carry on pointing to each word as you say it together; pointing helps you to keep time with each other.

At first you will have to find out what speed suits you both. If the child gets left behind, or misses out bits of words (or even whole words), slow down. If he is getting ahead of you, speed up a little. You will soon get used to each other and find that the right speed comes fairly naturally.

If you are having difficulty keeping together, it is usually helpful to slow down, and to read at first at a steady rhythm, as if you are reading in time with the sound of soldiers marching. You can then speed up and read with more expression as soon as you get used to reading together.

The commonest mistake in reading together is trying to go too fast. Take it steadily. Some adults naturally read very fast, and must make a conscious effort not to keep speeding up like a runaway train!

Make sure you do start difficult words at the same time as each other. Practise this, because it is very tempting to wait for each other when you come to a difficult word. Don't pause to see if the child is going to manage any of the words on his own, and don't ask him to 'sound out' any of the words.

If the child doesn't manage to read a word together with you – if he stops for you to say it first, misses it out, or doesn't get the word right – simply point to the word again, and try it again together. You will find he very quickly gets used to doing this. There is no need to tell him he's wrong, say 'no' or ask him to do anything else but try it again with you.

Sometimes when a parent and child can manage reading most words together, the child still lacks confidence in starting words he doesn't know at all at the same time as Mum; he often pauses when he reaches a problem word to let Mum go first. I find it helpful to demonstrate how reading together can help the child to get an unknown word right, first time. To do this, I ask the child to pick a word somewhere on the page that he doesn't know. Then I ask Mum and child to read together from the start of the sentence containing the tricky word – but not to stop, either of them, when they reach it. It can take a child a few goes at this (choosing a new tricky word each time) before he gathers up enough confidence to launch himself into the unknown word alongside Mum without stopping. This is however time well spent in building the confidence to make the best use of reading together in all the sessions to come. If you find that your child needs this extra training routine to overcome a tendency to stop at problem words when reading together, try it out a few times. Many children do not need the extra routine, but it is often surprisingly effective with those that do.

Plan to spend your second session as well as your first on practising reading together. Always start any paired reading session by reading together. Have short breaks during the session, and use them to refer to the hints in this section or (if you find it easier) in the summary at the end of the chapter. You may need more than two sessions before you feel comfortable at reading together – allow the extra practice time if you need it. As soon as you feel that both of you have 'got it together' without losing each other more than on the odd occasion, carry on to the next section.

Signalling

When you are happy with reading together, agree between you a suitable signal for your child to use to tell you he wants to read alone. I find a knock on the table, chair or other convenient surface is best – but anything like tapping his foot, the book (or you!) will do as well. You need a signal; the child simply asking you to stop reading together is no good because it would interrupt the reading.

Tell the child he can signal you to stop even if he only thinks he can manage a word or two on his own. Assure him that you will always come in again to help him as soon as he is stuck. He will take some time to get used to the idea of signalling, so expect quite a bit more reading together before he starts to signal. Don't worry about this – when he gets used to it, he will keep on doing it! In these early sessions you will need to encourage him to signal – at the beginning of each paragraph, suggest he tries a signal before the end of it, even if only to see what happens. Don't fall into the trap of stopping reading with him when he hasn't signalled, because you think its 'about time'. Be patient, and keep suggesting until he tries it.

When he signals, you a) stop reading with him, and b) praise him straight away for signalling (say, perhaps, 'good', 'thanks' or 'well done'). This is to encourage him to signal even more. His signal has now 'changed gear' for you both into reading alone.

Reading Alone

The child is now reading alone. Let him carry on reading to you. Listen carefully to what he is saying, and *keep up the patter of praise (feedback) all the time he is reading the words correctly*. Choose whatever praise (or feedback that he's doing OK) comes naturally. As we have already said, if you're not sure what words to use, use the words or 'positive noises' you make when somebody is telling you something interesting (listen to yourself and remember what responses you make!). Don't leave him in any doubt at any time that the word he has just read properly was right. Make especially sure that you praise him whenever he manages something particularly difficult like managing an especially tricky word, a word he usually gets wrong, a word he isn't sure is right (you can tell this by the questioning way he says it), or a string of words together that you didn't think he'd manage.

If he makes *any* mistake, point to the problem word to give him a chance to put it right. Do this if he reads a word wrongly or misses a word out. If he doesn't realize you want him to try it again, ask him to try it again. He will soon have a second try quite automatically when you point to a mistake, without you needing to say anything. Don't just let mistakes pass — point each mistake out for a second try.

When you've pointed to a mistake, or if he has simply got stuck and can't read the next word, count up four seconds to yourself. Don't try to prompt him, or ask him to sound it out, or make any other comment while he's struggling. If he's still struggling at the end of four seconds, *read the problem word together, and carry on reading together* until he signals again that he wants another try at reading alone. At the end of his 'four second try', lift your finger off the page and put it back under the word to signal that it is time to start reading together again, as you do at the beginning of each bit of reading together. You may need to remind him at first by saying something like 'read it with me'. It is important to read the problem word together (not just tell him what it is). If you don't succeed in getting it together, or he isn't confident enough to try it with you, tell him the word and then *repeat* it together. This is what you were doing whenever he didn't manage a word during reading together.

If the child does succeed in getting a word before his four seconds of effort is up, give him the praise or congratulations he's earned, and let him carry on reading alone.

I predict that you will forget to praise the child when he first reads alone in paired reading. Praise for reading, unless you are used to it, does not come naturally, and it will make you feel self-conscious to begin with. The secret is to start off by giving enough praise to make you glad no one else is watching, in case they made you feel somewhat silly doing it. As long as the words you use for praise are appropriate for your child, he will not find it at all silly.

Practising the Technique as a Whole

Once you have mastered the steps described so far, you are in a position to practise the whole of the technique. Always start off with reading together (so that the child is never left to read alone when he hasn't signalled) – remember to do this at the beginning of the day's session, or after you have had a short break or been interrupted in the middle of a session. Give yourselves short breaks to rest during your sessions; just a minute or so's rest from reading, perhaps discussing the story so far or looking at a picture in the book. A normal paired reading session will be made up of a number of spells of reading together with a number of spells of reading alone in between. Remember that the amount of time spent on each depends on how well the child can read, how difficult the book is, how confident he is at the time – and how tired he is. Reading alone will not happen frequently in the very earliest sessions, and will always be less with a more difficult book or when the child is lacking confidence or tired. Do not worry if you both spend most of the time reading together – he is learning all the time you are doing this.

On average, you will feel confident at paired reading after one to one and a half hours at it (four to six quarter-hour sessions or two to three half-hour sessions). While learning it, check your technique at the end of each session against the summary that follows this chapter. Refer to this during the early sessions whenever necessary.

One interesting point you will discover as you master paired reading is that you will not absorb or remember much of what you are both paired reading –

but your child will. The technique is designed so that the parent keeps the procedures going, while the child learns and enjoys the words being read, which is as it should be in helping a child read.

How Paired Reading will Develop Over Time

As you both become experienced at paired reading, a number of changes are likely to take place. Provided you avoid 'losing' the technique (see Chapter Six), these are likely to be:

(i) Increased speed of reading (but this can go too far – see Chapter Six on 'troubleshooting').

(ii) More fluent reading, during both reading together and reading alone – with better expression, pronunciation and attention paid to punctuation. It will sound more natural and like normal reading when the need to keep a steady rhythm to keep yourselves reading together has passed. You will no longer need to point all the time to keep the pace.

(iii) Praise/feedback coming more steadily and naturally, without you either having to think about it or feeling self-conscious.

(iv) Better understanding between you of exactly when to start the first word together and when a word needs a second try – you will no longer need to say 'with me' or similar requests, and just pointing to a word needing a second try will always be enough.

(v) The child no longer stopping when he reaches a tricky word during reading together.

(vi) More frequent signalling for reading alone.

(vii) The child signalling *immediately* he realizes he's made a mistake when reading alone, so that he stops you reading together for more than the one problem word (that must still be read together, though).

The last of these developments can be disconcerting if you're not ready for it – the child is wanting to change gear back to reading alone just as you're about to change into reading together! This is quite acceptable as long as you do both read the one problem word together before he carries on on his own.

SUMMARY OF PAIRED READING

1. Choose a book suitable for his age, that the child wants to read, regardless of being difficult for him.
2. Find somewhere quiet and sit side by side so that you can both see the book.
3. Start off reading aloud together, remember:
   - (i) read each word at exactly the same time as each other (not one after the other!)
   - (ii) if you 'lose' each other, or if the child misses bits out to keep up, *slow down*
   - (iii) point to the words to keep pace if you need to
   - (iv) if the child doesn't get a word with you, point to it again and try it again together
   - (v) don't slow down or stop reading to see if the child will manage on his own.
4. When the child signals (knocks) to try reading alone, you:
   - (i) stop reading to let him carry on alone
   - (ii) praise him for signalling
   - (iii) keep up a 'patter' of praise/feedback all the time he is reading correctly
   - (iv) point to any mistakes and ask him to have one more try at it
   - (v) don't ask him to sound words out.
5. Whenever he can't correct a mistake in four seconds, *or* if he is stuck for four seconds, you:
   - (i) read the problem word together (tell him what it is first if he can't manage it with you)
   - (ii) carry on reading together again until his next signal to read alone.
6. Always start off by reading together.
7. Aim at a quarter of an hour's session each day.
8. Change books whenever he wants.
9. A more difficult book will keep you in 'reading together' gear for more of the time – this is quite in order.

Remember that paired reading is like driving a car with two gears – 'reading together' gear and 'reading alone' gear. The child changes you both into reading alone gear by signalling when he wants to. You change back into reading together gear whenever he is stuck for four seconds.

FIVE: MONITORING PAIRED READING

Some parents and teachers will be happy to use paired reading on the basis of its record to date, without specifically measuring any progress being made. Monitoring the child's reading skill is however important when one is using a technique aimed at changing it. Measuring progress may show clear improvement (which doesn't *prove* that this is the result of one's extra efforts, but which certainly suggests continuing with paired reading for the child concerned). It may show success which then tails off (suggesting a break from extra reading sessions, or, if the tailing off happens when the child's reading is still very poor, the need to consider further types of specialist help). It may show that no progress is being made (which suggests that either the technique is not being used properly, or that paired reading is not appropriate for the child concerned).

In addition to measurement of any improvement in reading, it is also vital to monitor paired reading sessions themselves to check that the technique is still being used properly. If it is not, its effects can be lost.

This chapter describes ways of measuring or assessing improvement in reading, and of checking that paired reading is being used correctly. If you are a parent using this handbook without backup supervision, the chapter should guide you on monitoring in both these ways for yourself. If you are a teacher running a home/school reading scheme, it will provide the means for your own monitoring of the paired reading being carried out by parents on the scheme.

It is not suggested that everyone should carry out all the monitoring methods described in this chapter. It is however suggested that parents or teachers should select and use one method of monitoring reading, and also monitor the use of the technique. If you are prepared to invest your time, and the child's, in reading sessions at home, it is worth checking properly whether it is working.

BASELINE TESTING

To measure a child's improvement in reading, it is necessary to measure his reading skill before starting paired reading. If you don't measure the starting point, there is nothing to compare later measurements with and thus no way of determining clearly whether he has improved. The most basic method used by researchers to find out how much a skill has improved is to measure the skill before trying to improve it (the baseline test), to measure it again after trying to improve it, and then to take one measurement from the other to see how much improvement occurred between the tests.

MEASURING IMPROVEMENT IN READING

There are a number of ways of assessing reading performance for both baseline measurement before paired reading, and later measurements to compare with this to check progress. Some are more accurate and objective than others. If you are a parent helping your own child, you will not have reading tests to use, but you can use the other approaches outlined below. If you are a teacher, consideration should be given to using reading tests. If you are doing research on paired reading, not only will you need reading tests, but it would be advisable to use a number of measures to check more than one aspect of reading (and avoid being too affected by the limitations of one particular measurement or test). The researcher should also compare the results of a group of children using paired reading with those of a 'control' group of similar children not using paired reading (to check what improvement would have happened anyway, without paired reading).

Means of assessing reading, and improvement in it are:

Reading Tests
Most standard, published reading tests can be used to give a baseline measurement of reading skill, usually as a reading age. Such tests however are not usually designed to be used again after only a short time to check progress, so that while they do give an objective measure of progress, there is a built-in margin of error as well. A test much used so far in evaluating paired reading, which is widely available and easily used by teachers, is the Neale Analysis of Reading Ability.

Because formal reading tests were not designed for frequent re-use, they are not suitable for weekly or fortnightly monitoring (in many cases, one would end up measuring how well the child was memorizing the test!). Reading tests come into their own as 'before and after' measures; at least two months, and preferably three months or more, should elapse between the baseline and the 'after' test. Tests are useful for assessing the overall effects of a course of, say, three months of paired reading, but do not satisfy the parent's need for a continuing guide on how the child is doing.

Using a 'Progress Book'
One way of assessing regularly how a child's reading is progressing is to use a 'progress book'. This is a book the child is interested in but which is kept aside for progress-testing only – it is not used for paired reading. As with the books which are being used for paired reading, the progress book should be appropriate for the child's actual (rather than reading) age. If the child has chosen for paired reading a book which is one of a series, another book from the same series makes an ideal progress book. Another book by the same author and aimed at the same age group is also ideal.

To measure the child's ability to read the progress book, ask him to read a passage of exactly a hundred words aloud to you (count them up first). He can be praised for correct reading, but when testing (as opposed to paired reading) simply tell him the right word each time he makes a mistake or gets stuck for four seconds. Count the number of times he does make a mistake or gets stuck (keep a tally on a piece of scrap paper while he is reading), then take the total from a hundred to give his score of words read correctly out of a hundred.

Use the progress book to take a baseline measurement before you start paired reading, then make further assessments every week to check whether his score of words read correctly is improving or not. Use a different passage of a hundred words each time – and don't cheat by letting him practise reading the progress book!

Unlike a reading test, assessments with a progress book do not give you a reading age, and this type of measurement is a little rough and ready because it does assume that the progress book is approximately the same level of difficulty all the way through. (That is, if he scores better on one passage of a hundred words than the one he read a few weeks ago, we are assuming this is because he can now read better, rather than because he has reached an easier part of the book.) A different progress book would probably produce very different scores. However, weekly checks with a progress book are very satisfactory indeed for easy use at home, and will give a useful assessment of whether paired reading is actually improving his reading.

Avoiding Unwanted Variations

When assessing improvement with a progress book, expect the scores to vary quite markedly up and down from one week to the next – what matters is whether the child's scores are improving generally over time. You can iron out some of the unwanted variations by avoiding irrelevant factors that may affect scores – such as how tired the child is. Try to use the progress book at the same time of day each week, avoid distractions (which may lower his score), and avoid assessing progress on days which are very different from normal (e.g. after late nights, outings or on birthdays). Also try not to test when one of you is in a bad mood!

Using a Graph
To see whether there is, or is not, a steady improvement regardless of the ups and downs from one week to the next, plot each week's scores on a graph.

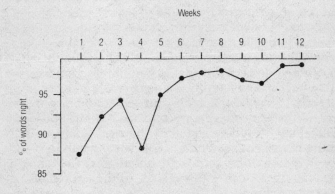

FIGURE ONE: Progress Graph showing °₀ of words right each week

After a number of weeks, it will become easy to see what is happening to reading skill. If the graph shows a general trend towards better scores over the weeks, it is a safe assumption that this is because the child's reading is improving, rather than because the progress book is getting steadily easier to read! Figure One shows the graph of scores produced by one of the first children to use paired reading: note the obvious improvement over time, and also the frequent ups and downs in scores.

Measuring Progress during Paired Reading Sessions
It is tricker, but quite possible, to measure the child's skill at reading correctly during normal paired reading sessions rather than separate weekly sessions with a progress book. To do this, tape-record the first part of the

session — until you are sure he has read at least a hundred words during 'reading alone'. Then after the session, replay the tape, and count all the mistakes, and occasions during those hundred words when you had started reading together again because he was stuck. Take care to count mistakes you pointed out, even if he managed to correct them on his second try. Again, repeat this weekly to give you scores which can be plotted on a graph to see if he is progressing.

This way of assessing progress can be laborious, because you will probably have to replay the tape twice (once to count the first hundred words alone and again to count mistakes and getting stuck). This can take as long as having a separate session with a progress book. You may however prefer it if you have a tape recorder and you may be recording some paired reading sessions anyway to keep a check on your technique (see below).

It is theoretically possible to keep a tally of words read alone, mistakes and getting stuck, while actually doing the paired reading session with the child. Don't try it. Attempting to do all this at the same time as keeping up your praise/feedback to the child, and responding properly to his mistakes or problems while reading alone, is too much. One or another of the tasks will suffer as a result.

Ratings of Progress
So far we have concentrated on measures of progress which are fairly accurate and objective, but which concentrate on reading words correctly. There is more to reading than getting words right, however, and some important aspects of progress are not so easily counted or measured. One can make use of one's own judgement, and that of the child concerned, in monitoring progress, as well as using tests and counts of correct words. To be useful, the judgements made must be recorded regularly, and in a way that allows a comparison to be made between one judgement and the next (the 'before and after' issue again). The most straightforward method of recording and comparing

judgements about how different aspects of reading are (or are not) progressing, is by using ratings.

To monitor progress by ratings; (i) select which aspects of reading are to be monitored (a list of key aspects is given below – others can be added), (ii) choose who is to rate each aspect (parent, teacher, child, or a combination of these), (iii) every two weeks, the appropriate person should decide on what the position is for each aspect and give it a rating out of 5 (see below), (iv) write the ratings down for each aspect and (v) compare the ratings (or put them on a graph) over a period to check progress. Figure Two shows a convenient chart for recording ratings.

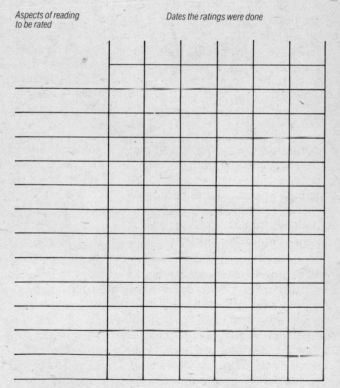

Aspects of reading to be rated   Dates the ratings were done

FIGURE TWO: Record Chart for Ratings

Every two weeks, put the rating number that has been given for each aspect of reading in the appropriate box. Check progress by comparing the ratings that have been given each time with the ones given before.

Don't cheat by looking at the chart before you decide on your ratings – looking to see what you gave last time may influence your choice this time! Do your comparing with last time *after* you've decided on your new ratings.

The list below gives key aspects of reading which may be selected for monitoring by means of rating, together with guidance on deciding the rating from 0 to 4 (i.e. a rating scale of 5 points):

1. *Expression* in the way the child reads alone – rating by parent or teacher, scoring;

No expression at all	0
Poor expression	1
Reasonable expression	2
Good expression	3
Excellent expression	4

2. Following the *punctuation* when reading alone – rating by parent or teacher, scoring;

Ignores punctuation	0
Follows punctuation poorly	1
Follows punctuation reasonably well	2
Follows punctuation very well	3
Follows punctuation extremely well	4

3. Whether he *reads things* (books, comics, signs, labels etc) *of his own accord*, when not asked to – rating by parent, scoring;

Reads nothing of his own accord	0
Reads very little of his own accord	1
Reads a fair amount of his own accord	2
Reads a lot of his own accord	3
Reads a very large amount of his own accord	4

4. His *speed of reading* alone — rating by parent or
   teacher, scoring;
   Reads much too slowly   −2
   Reads a little too slowly   −1
   Reads at an acceptable speed   0
   Reads a little too fast   +1
   Reads much too fast   +2
(note that this time higher scores are not good — the
aim is a '0' score, and plus or minus ratings show the
need to adjust to a more normal speed).

5. The *child's view of paired reading* — rating by the
   child, scoring;
   I hate it   −2
   I don't like it   −1
   I don't really like or dislike it   0
   I like it   +1
   I like it a lot   +2

6. The *child's view of the book* being read — rating by
   the child, scoring;
   I hate it   −2
   I don't like it   −1
   I don't really like or dislike it   0
   I like it   +1
   I like it a lot   +2
(Note; for both of these ratings by the child, he may
have views for or against — if he stays disliking the
book, change books. If he stays disliking Paired
Reading, try to find out why, but in any case give him a
break from it for a while.)

7. *Learning during paired reading of words he doesn't
   know* — rating by parent or teacher, scoring;
   No words he didn't already know
   are being learned   0
   Very few words are being learned   1
   Some words are being learned   2
   Many words are being learned   3
   Very many words are being learned   4

8. Judgement of *overall progress* – rating by parent, teacher and child, scoring;

Reading skill is getting much worse	-2
Reading skill is getting a little worse	-1
Reading skill is staying the same	0
Reading skill is getting a little better	$+1$
Reading skill is getting much better	$+2$

Note that more than one or two minus scores on the last rating above may indicate a more serious problem than the temporary setbacks that do occur from time to time. If two minus scores are given in a row, (i) begin monitoring with a progress book as well to check more objectively what is happening (ii) note in what way reading is judged to be getting worse, (iii) check that paired reading is being used properly and (iv) arrange for parent and teacher to compare notes on their judgements of progress, or lack of it. If the rating seems correct and there is still no progress after this, stop paired reading and consider a specialist assessment. If paired reading is to be tried again after a break, or together with another form of reading help, monitor progress with a progress book and/or reading tests.

Comprehension

As well as reading words correctly, a reader needs to understand what is being read. Paired Reading has a good record of improving children's comprehension as well as their accuracy of reading – it encourages words to be read correctly *and* to sink in.

It is worth considering a measurement or rating of comprehension amongst the possible means of monitoring progress in reading. There are three basic ways of doing this. Firstly, a teacher can use the comprehension questions that form part of some reading tests. Secondly, a parent or teacher can ask some questions (not too many – more a brief quiz) after a paired reading session, once every one or two weeks to check how much the child has understood from what he read during the session. This can then be rated, according to the child's answers, scoring 0 for no understanding of what he has read, 1 for very little understanding, 2 for a fair understanding, 3 for a good understanding, and 4 for an excellent understanding. These ratings can then be compared over the weeks to check progress, as with ratings of other aspects of reading.

The third means of monitoring comprehension, particularly with an older child or teenager, is to ask the child to make a rating every two or three weeks of how well he is able to understand what he is paired reading.

CHECKING THAT PAIRED READING IS BEING DONE CORRECTLY

Like car driving, one's paired reading technique can deteriorate over time and inappropriate habits can creep in. It is far from easy to notice this for oneself while doing paired reading – you need to listen to a session being done and note whether the various aspects of the technique are being used correctly. It is particularly important for a parent working without supervision or backup to check regularly that the technique is still being used properly.

A teacher can monitor how parents are using the technique in a home/school reading scheme by listening to, and checking, a short session of paired reading at regular intervals – preferably at least once a fortnight.

A parent can monitor her own use of paired reading by tape-recording a session (or part of a session) each week and then checking that the technique is correct while playing it back later. Alternatively, you can ask someone else in the family who knows how to do paired reading to listen to you doing it and check your technique for you.

Provided that you are both happy doing it, there is no reason why the child himself shouldn't help to check how well you are using the technique together when playing back a tape-recording of a session.

To check the use of the technique, whether you are a teacher or other adult listening to a 'check session' or you are a parent checking yourself with a tape recorder, go through the checklist given below. These are things that should be happening during paired reading. Adjust what is being done accordingly.

PAIRED READING CHECKLIST

1. Use a book the child has chosen.
2. Use a book suitable for the child's actual, rather than reading age.
3. Do paired reading for a quarter of an hour each day.
4. Always start off by 'reading together'.
5. While reading together, say each word at the same time as each other.
6. Avoid stopping in order to see if the child can manage on his own.
7. Point to each word with your finger to keep pace together, if necessary.
8. Point again to words that are not read properly together, and try again.
9. Stop reading when the child signals, letting him carry on alone.
10. Praise him for signalling.
11. Keep up a patter of praise/feedback while he is reading alone correctly.
12. Point out mistakes to give him a second try.
13. Avoid asking him to sound words out.
14. Start reading together with him after four seconds if he is stuck.
15. Say together any word he was stuck on.
16. Keep reading together after coming in to help, unless and until he signals.

Checking the Sessions

It is helpful to keep a simple record of when paired reading sessions are done, both to check on how long has been spent on paired reading over the weeks, and as an encouragement to keep the sessions up. Having to note down too many missed sessions helps to counter any tendencies to let the effort fizzle out!

A simple way of recording when sessions are done is

to mark a diary or calendar each day a session is held at home. A more detailed record can be kept on a chart such as that illustrated in Figure Three.

RECORD CHART

DATE STARTED:

Put number of minutes reading (to the nearest 5)
Put "x" for a missed day

WEEKS:	1	2	3	4	5	6	7	8	9	10	11	12
Sunday												
Monday												
Tuesday												
Wednesday												
Thursday												
Friday												
Saturday												

FIGURE THREE: Record of reading sessions

This can also be used to note the length of each session. Teachers using paired reading on home/school schemes will find such charts useful in monitoring the work being done at home. Over a number of weeks, some families may be expected to put in far more, and others far less time on reading than a quarter of an hour per day.

DECIDING ON HOW TO MONITOR

This chapter has suggested a wide range of monitoring methods, and there are others that might have been added. It would be overdoing things to try too many at once. Different parents and different teachers will be interested in monitoring different aspects of improvement, or guarding against different possible problems, and will settle for different levels of accuracy and objectivity in their monitoring. These factors will influence which monitoring methods are chosen.

A basic monitoring 'package' for parental use would be a fortnightly rating of overall progress, a note on the calendar when sessions are held, and a weekly check using the list provided above with the aid of a tape recorder. The parent wishing to be more precise may substitute weekly use of a progress book instead of an overall rating, and may add other aspects to be rated.

The teacher monitoring a number of parents and children on a scheme may give reading tests before and after a 'course' of paired reading, ask parents to keep a chart of sessions held, and at fortnightly checkup sessions (at school or at the child's home) listen to a sample of parent and child doing paired reading to advise on any changes needed. To this may be added use of a progress book for more precise monitoring, and ratings of factors of particular interest or concern.

A final comment is necessary on the frequency of monitoring. Paired reading has been used for 'courses' of many different lengths, but a three-month course is a reasonable period to start with and to expect to produce a significant improvement in reading. (It can of course be continued indefinitely if all is going well.) Reading tests can (just) be used before and after this period. Because variations in scores are likely, a progress book needs to be used weekly to give enough scores to show clearly what is happening. On the other hand, ratings are better if not done too frequently (not more than every two weeks), otherwise there is a tendency to keep giving the same rating and not to notice (or even perhaps to expect) changes between one rating and the next.

SIX: TROUBLESHOOTING

The greatest risk in learning a technique from a book is that no one is available to help solve any problems. It is a shortcoming only too familiar to anyone who has tried D.I.Y. car repairs with only a handbook in support! This chapter aims to provide solutions to the more common problems that parents and children may come across in using paired reading – it gives the advice I most often find is needed during my own 'check-up' sessions with families. To anyone who comes across a difficulty not mentioned or resolved by this usual range of problems and solutions, I can but apologize.

Dislike of Reading Sessions

Although many children with reading problems have built up a dislike of extra reading, it is very rare for a child to dislike doing paired reading once he has tried it. If he does, check that he really is keen on the book chosen, allow him to try *any* reading material he shows a flicker of interest in (provided it's not something so terrible you decide to ban it), and check that reading sessions are not displacing a favourite activity (advice was given in Chapter Four on this). If he really is against reading sessions, try firstly learning the technique together (if you are careful to make the learning enjoyable he may find it's not as bad as he expected) and then phasing sessions in gradually – five minutes every other day, then five minutes each day, increase to ten minutes a day, and finally increase to fifteen. Outline this plan to him, explaining that it is taking his reluctance into account and agree not to overload him, only increasing his 'daily dose' when he is happy with the previous 'dose'. In extremis, and if you find the idea acceptable, you could consider agreeing a deal with him, such as a contract which allows some benefit like extra T.V. in return for so much reading work. Such a deal will seem reasonable in some families, when perhaps other reluctantly done tasks like mowing the lawn or doing the washing up are linked to some payoff in return. It will not be at all acceptable to other families, and so not a possible strategy to use.

If a child remains adamant that he does not want to do paired reading (or any other form of reading at home, for that matter), *do not force him*. Beware the old adage that you can force a horse to water but you can't make him drink. Forcing him to do it will (a) not improve his reading and (b) put him off reading even more. Give him a break from the issue, and try again in three months' time. It may help then to try under different circumstances (perhaps holiday time rather than term time, or vice versa) and with the other parent for a change. Not only is it rare for a child to dislike paired reading; it is rarer for a child to carry on disliking it when it is tried again.

Loss of Interest
Children's interest in many activities tends to come and go in phases, and reading sessions are no exception. It is wise to plan a course of paired reading for a definite period (say three months) and then have a break before the next stint if interest is flagging. You can of course keep going if the interest is well sustained. During a course of paired reading, the best countermeasure to loss of interest is a wide choice of books, plus efforts to borrow or buy any book the child is especially interested in, or which tallies with his current interests.

Problem Choice of Books
Some children choose books for paired reading which may seem unsuitable, despite the guidance already given. Books with captions and speech in 'balloons' over the characters' heads are perfectly suitable (if sometimes wearing for the adult!). Very difficult books are usually suitable, even though the child may have to

stay 'reading together' for most of the time. Two indicators that the book really is too hard and that something slightly easier is needed are, firstly, if the child does not signal to read alone at all during a typical fifteen minute session, and secondly if he cannot manage a number of the words correctly with you during reading together.

A much more common problem than the too-difficult book is that many children will choose too easy a book. There is also the temptation for adults to go along with this. The child has become conditioned to reading only simple books, and is used to finding anything more difficult both impossible to manage, and stressful to try. An over-easy book is therefore often chosen at the beginning of paired reading, before the child has found out for himself that he is going to be able to cope with more difficult fare.

It does not matter if the child and parent learn paired reading on an easy book, but once all is going well, encourage the child to be more adventurous. The main indication that the book is too easy is when the child can spend a whole session reading alone and never needing to read together, and being able to correct any mistakes as soon as they are pointed out. If the child isn't stretched at all by the book, he is practising but not learning much that is new.

Note that you only need to switch to a more challenging book if the easy one is one written for younger children. There will come a time, if all goes well, when the child can read a book written for his own age without needing much help from reading together, and he will therefore keep going alone. You do not need to keep upping the level of difficulty beyond his own age level. There is however no reason why he should not use the assistance of paired reading to read something more adult if he wants to.

Wandering Attention

This is a common problem. The child starts to look at the pictures or round the room, gives up signalling to read alone, and during reading together either 'echoes' you without looking at the book, or you find yourself left reading all on your own. The most common cause of this is a tired child, and the best immediate solution is to give up today and try again tomorrow at a time when he's less tired.

To minimize the problem, paired read at times of day other than the evenings if possible, and allow frequent (but short) breaks during sessions.

The almost surefire solution if the problem persists is for the child rather than the adult to point to the words as they are read. The pace may become a little ragged, but you cannot point to the words if your attention is wandering somewhere else.

Ignoring Punctuation

This is common in early readers, and usually improves with overall reading skill and experience. To encourage improvement, explain what the punctuation marks mean, follow them yourself while reading together so that the child practises following the punctuation with you, and praise him when he responds to punctuation while reading alone. Asking him to slow down if he's reading too fast will help.

Frequent 'Careless Mistakes'

If paired reading is being done properly, all mistakes made will be corrected as a matter of course. As was pointed out earlier, mistakes are often more likely on simple words than more complex ones, and this isn't an indication of carelessness.

Some children however will race at almost breakneck speed when reading alone, particularly once there has been a definite improvement in their reading skill. While going too fast, they will make numerous small errors. The solution is simply to slow them down by insisting that they read alone at a pace you set by pointing to the words.

'Drifting' away from the Instructions

This is less of a problem than a warning. There is a tendency for one's use of any detailed technique to 'drift' away from following the original instructions after one has been doing it for some time. This happens with many techniques – instructions get forgotten, shortcuts are taken, some of one's own ideas get added, and some bad habits are introduced. Often, one does not realize how far one has drifted from the original procedures, and reading techniques for parents and children are no exception.

The danger of drifting away from the paired reading instructions is that although you may not realize that you have changed the technique significantly, you may have destroyed its benefits for your child. One research study,[1] aimed at comparing different ways of parents helping children read at home, found that almost all the parents drifted away from the techniques they had been asked to use. They had ended up doing the same thing – listening to the child reading aloud – instead. The result was that none of the techniques (including paired reading) they had started with could produce any significant benefits. Where parents do keep using paired reading, researchers have reported very significant benefits (see Chapter Eight).

An example of less dramatic problems arising from drifting away from the original technique occurred the evening before I wrote this section, at one of my regular paired reading sessions with parents and children at a local primary school. A girl who has been progressing extremely well with paired reading came to the session with an unusually difficult leaflet to read, to show me how well she was doing. She and Mum tried to paired read the leaflet – but soon ended up in confusion and unable to cope with it. The reason was a simple drifting from the instructions. On their usual book, the child spent most of the time reading alone, and had always signalled Mum to stop reading together after being helped with only one word. The drift away from the instructions was that Mum had become used

1 Lorraine Wareing: A Comparative Study of three methods of parental involvement in reading. M.Sc. thesis, North East London Polytechnic.

to only reading together for one word whenever there was a problem, and had formed the habit of always stopping after one word together, whether or not her daughter had signalled. To make matters worse, the girl had given up signalling, because Mum always stopped anyway. The result – on a more difficult piece of reading, the 'reading together' help did not carry on when the child did need it, and they could not read the leaflet. They had dropped out of paired reading its ability to adapt to more difficult reading material. (Pointing out the importance of signalling, even after only one word each time, solved the problem, and they then read the leaflet successfully.)

The countermeasure to drifting away from the instructions is monitoring the technique regularly, as outlined in Chapter Five. If you find that monitoring isn't happening regularly, *at least* re-read the checklist at the end of Chapter Five each week to remind yourself of the rules. All the elements in paired reading are there for a purpose, and your child may need each one of them, now or later on.

Keeping Pace while Reading Together

It has already been suggested that if it proves difficult to read absolutely together, parent and child can read at a steady rhythm (about the pace of marching soldiers) and the parent can point to each word as it is to be read. This should later allow you to progress to more fluent, less rhythmic reading.

If it does not, tips on keeping pace together without always sounding like robots or marching feet are as follows. Firstly, make sure you start off exactly together, by counting 'one, two, three . . .' before you start if necessary. Secondly, keep the pace slower than either of you normally read. Thirdly, give a generous pause for any coughs or other 'natural interruptions' from either of you, and again if necessary, count 'one, two, three . . .' before carrying on. Fourthly, point to each syllable (rather than each complete word) as it is to be said together – you will find that this enables you to read more fluently and take more notice of punctuation than keeping a strict rhythm does. Finally, check that the book is not being jogged by your finger 'stabbing' the page, and that you are not covering up words the child needs to see with your hand. These are simple, but often overlooked problems. I find it helpful to let the child rather than the adult hold the book to see if he finds it easier to see it and keep pace then. It is also often helpful to point to words from above them rather than below them (so that if your hand is covering anything up, it's words you've already read rather than those that are to come).

The Child who Doesn't Signal

Most children have this problem at first; it is extremely rare for it to persist after the first few sessions. If it does, remind and encourage the child to signal whenever you start a new paragraph (but *don't* stop reading together unless he does, and don't get impatient with him – that won't help if he's already lacking confidence). Ask him to choose what signal he would like to use (anything that doesn't interfere with the flow of reading will do). Some children are happier using one signal than another. Praise him when he does signal (*don't* say 'about time too'!). If all else fails, switch to an easier book to make reading alone both easier and more likely, and to boost the child's confidence that he can cope with the book in front of him.

Tutors with Reading Problems

It has already been said that a parent (or even another child) with reading problems themselves can still help a child by paired reading with him. Important points are: the tutor and child concerned must be happy at the idea of working together on reading; the tutor must be a better reader than the child (by at least two years of reading age); the tutor must explain to the child that he or she may get stuck too – and when this happens, accept that neither can read the word so leave it at that (*don't* just guess at it). Working together on reading

87

when it is a problem for both of you can be a great confidence booster. A recently discovered (and unexpected) bonus of paired reading is that it can help the *tutor* as well as the child, to improve his or her reading skills.

Different Accents

I began paired reading in Birmingham, and one of the volunteer tutors on the first scheme had a strong Irish accent. I have fond recollections of a combination of Irish and Brummie accents reading together! Accent should not be a problem to parents paired reading with their own children, but teachers, those not working with their own children, and children tutoring other children may find accents both different and unfamiliar. The guideline is that if the tutor and child can easily understand each other's speech, they will have no problems paired reading – but people who find it hard to understand each other anyway will have problems paired reading together. Sometimes it is helpful for the tutor to pronounce certain words the child's way (e.g. pronouncing the word 'the' as 'thee' or 'thuh').

Problems at Particular Ages

Paired reading, although suitable for virtually all ages, does have to take children's ages into account. Two common age-related problems are the very young child who wants to paired read the same book all the time, and the teenager who is touchy about praise. With the very young child, it is quite acceptable for him to use a book he already knows by heart – this is an excellent book to learn the technique with, and it is the way very young children like to use reading. Encourage him to try new reading material as well (not instead) when he has learned the technique with you.

The older teenager is likely to be quite anti reading sessions. There is no special solution to this – but make the most of paired reading's possibilities. Use adult reading material (the sports page of the newspaper is fine if he wants to read it), in line with his interests (why not a motorcycle maintenance manual?). Be careful to use the term 'feedback' rather than praise (the same effects with a more acceptable label), and concentrate on words like 'yes' and 'correct'.

Changing Tutor

As long as both tutors follow the paired reading rules, changes of tutor should not cause problems. Confusion will however occur if either one tutor has drifted away from the instructions, or if a new tutor does not learn the technique properly. In both cases, the answer is simple. Follow and monitor the instructions. In changing tutor (or where more than one tutor is working with the child), it is helpful for a second tutor to watch the first for a while, to pick up details of pace, type of signalling, and so on.

If you have made a significant change in your work with the child – a change of tutor or change in time of session perhaps – it is useful to check any effects on reading accuracy on a graph of scores from a progress book (see the previous chapter). You may find that trying a particular solution to a problem affects the child's reading accuracy; if so, it matters in which direction.

SEVEN: VARIATIONS AND OTHER TECHNIQUES FOR PARENTS

Just as there is a growing trend in education, for parents to become involved in helping their children to read, so the number of techniques and variations on techniques for parents to use is also growing. My aim in this chapter is to give an idea of the current range of approaches, as the background against which paired reading can be considered. There are three main types of approach; variations on paired reading itself, other parent-helping techniques, and the special children's books that are increasingly appearing in the bookshops, specially written for parents and children to read together at home. I have quoted the published sources of variations where appropriate. The terms 'Three Stage reading' and 'Five Stage reading' are my own description of these particular variations on the paired reading theme.

VARIATIONS ON PAIRED READING
A number of teachers and researchers have produced adaptations to paired reading, sometimes with the aim of discovering a more effective or more easily used version, and sometimes to simplify it even further for very young children. The major variations so far described in various publications are:

Three Stage Reading
(See Bryans, T., Kidd, A., and Levey, M., 'The Kings Heath Project' in the book *Parental Involvement in Children's Reading* edited by Keith Topping and Sheila Wolfendale, published in 1985 by Croom Helm.) This variation differs from paired reading itself in reading

the same passage in a number of different ways, and in abandoning the usual ways of changing from reading together to reading alone and back again (thus there is no signalling and no 'four-second rule'). Instead, the parent reads a few lines to the child, then they read the same lines together, then the child reads the lines again, alone (while the parent gives praise and corrects mistakes). Using this technique, children's reading accuracy has been found to improve significantly, but not their comprehension of what they are reading.

Five Stage Reading
(See Young, P., and Tyre, C., *Dyslexia or Illiteracy?*, The Open University Press, 1983.)

This variation divides helping the child into a greater number of stages, but still includes the three stages outlined above, and again leaves out signalling and the four-second rule. The five stages are; 1) parent and child discuss the passage to be read, 2) the parent reads the passage to the child for three minutes, 3) parent and child read the same passage aloud together, 4) parent and child again read the passage aloud together – but this time the parent stops occasionally to leave the child to carry on reading a word or phrase alone, and 5) the child reads the same passage alone (the parent correcting mistakes). Children's reading improved significantly in a one year long project using this variation of paired reading.

Beginning Readers Variation
(See Gillham, B., 'Paired Reading in Perspective', in *Child Education*, 1986.)

This is the variation of paired reading set out in the 'Paired Reading Storybooks' series published by Methuen for very young children beginning to read (rather than older children needing help with their reading). There are four main changes from the original form of paired reading: 1) instead of the child deciding when he wants to try reading alone and signalling his parent to stop reading with him, the parent decides when to drop out – lowering her voice and then stopping altogether to leave the child reading on his own; 2) instead of a free choice of books, the child is offered a selected range of books judged likely to be suitable; 3) parents are not asked to praise the child for reading alone correctly, and 4) the same book is read a number of times over. Detailed results of this version of paired reading are not available, but Gillham does report improvements in reading from its use in one pair of schools.

Prepared Reading
(See Tyre, C., and Young, P., 'Parents as coaches for dyslexic and severely reading-retarded pupils' in the book *Parental Involvement in Children's Reading.*)

This variation has been suggested as a development of paired reading suitable for children with a reading age over 8. In prepared reading, parent and child first discuss the passage to be read, then the parent reads it aloud to the child; the child then reads it silently to himself (asking for help if necessary) before finally reading it aloud. The authors of this approach did not give information on its effectiveness.

Shared Reading
(See Greening, M., and Spenceley, J., 'Shared Reading: a review of the Cleveland Project,' InPsych (Bulletin of the Cleveland County Psychological Service), Vol 11, No 1, 1984.)

Shared reading is basically the 'reading together' part of paired reading, without the rest of the technique. It is therefore a very much simpler version of the procedure, intended to be used from the very earliest stage of starting to read. It is also intended to avoid the possibility of making mistakes even more than normal paired reading does (with no reading alone, the child does not try words on his own, and so cannot make mistakes). The use of only part of the paired reading procedure is that much easier for parents to learn and do. Results so far show significant improvements in reading accuracy following shared reading with children aged 5 to 8.

Comment on Paired Reading Variations

All the techniques listed so far have been described as variations of the original form of paired reading. You may find one of these particularly attractive – but remember that they do not have as many research reports on their effectiveness as the original form of paired reading does.

The 'three stage' version of paired reading is interesting in that it appears to produce good improvements in the accuracy of reading, as paired reading itself does, but without the bonus of better understanding to go with the better accuracy. The original form of paired reading described in this handbook normally produces even greater improvements in the child's comprehension than in his accuracy of reading (see Chapter Eight).

Two of the variations – shared reading and Gillham's version for beginning readers – aim to make paired reading easier and more natural for the younger child at the starting reading (rather than remedial reading) stage. Both do this by leaving out parts of normal paired reading. Gillham leaves out the child signalling, suggesting instead that the parent should judge when to leave the child to carry on on his own (Young and Tyre do much the same in their 'five stage' version). Your particular child may prefer this – if so, fine. It does however carry the risk of the parent judging when to drop out wrongly and leaving the child without help when, given the choice, he would have preferred to keep the help there. I have never found it necessary to advise parents to drop out without the usual signal from the child; even very young children soon pick up the idea of 'knocking' to stop the parent for a bit, and even those who (at any age) are reluctant signallers at first eventually start signalling quite happily. Dropping out without the child signalling you to drop out, takes away the child's guarantee that he has help *all* the time he wants it.

Although Gillham does not ask parents to use praise when children are successfully reading alone, praise is known to be so effective in assisting learning, and young children are especially responsive to it, that it is well worth keeping the praise element in any technique for helping beginning readers to read.

Shared reading is in some ways opposite to Gillham's version of paired reading in trying to simplify things for the very early reader. Far from the adult dropping out to leave the child reading on his own, in shared reading the adult never drops out at all, with or without a signal from the child. The results its users report for shared reading are important – they indicate that the 'reading together' part of paired reading, even on its own, helps children to read. A small research study by Heath (published in 1981 in *Edition 2*, the journal of the Inner London Education Authority School Psychological Service) showed that the reading of a group of children also improved with just the 'praise while reading alone' half of paired reading. Heath found better improvement when both reading together and reading alone were used. Although some of the research studies are small, nevertheless it seems on the basis of what is known so far that *both* reading alone and reading together can help children read. Full paired reading brings both 'big guns' to bear on improving the child's reading.

As a final comment in this section, it is important to stress that paired reading 'proper' has been found both usable and effective in helping 5 and 6 year olds learning to read for the first time, without any of the technique having to be left out.

OTHER PARENT-HELPING TECHNIQUES
Some of the main alternatives to paired reading are briefly described in this chapter, together with published sources of information about them. As well as the techniques that have been published, many

parents for many years, have worked out their own ways of helping their particular children read. Some of these are highly effective for the child concerned, some not so – but without trying them out on large numbers of children and measuring the results, one cannot say which are worth trying and which are not. The key in choosing how to help your child to read is to check how effective it has proved to be with other children.

Listening to Children Read

A research study by Dr Jenny Hewison in Dagenham, London, showed that 7 year olds whose parents regularly listened to them read at home were definitely better at reading than children who did not have this help at home. (See Hewison, J., and Tizard, J., 'Parental Involvement and Reading Attainment', in *British Journal of Educational Psychology*, 1980, Vol 50, pages 209–215.) The well known 'Haringey Project' that followed confirmed that listening to children reading improves their reading skills (see Tizard, J., Schofield, W. N., and Hewison, J., 'Collaboration between Teachers and parents in Assisting Children's Reading', in *British Journal of Educational Psychology*, 1982, Vol 52, pages 1–15). What parents were asked to do was simply to listen to their children reading aloud, and when the child was stuck, to wait a short while and then give the word or correct the mistake. Parents who wished to, could prompt the child when he was stuck. No special techniques were used.

Another well known project which found good results from parents listening to children read was the 'Belfield Project' in which over a hundred children regularly read to their parents at home (see Hannon, P., Jackson, A., and Page, B., 'Implementation and take-up of a project to involve parents in the teaching of reading', in the book *Parental Involvement in Children's Reading*).

Praise and Rewards

The importance of praise in encouraging correct reading has already been stressed. Some reading researchers have taken this one step further, and added small 'prizes' to reinforce correct reading. (For examples, see Staats, A. W., 'Behaviour analysis and token reinforcement in educational behaviour modification and curriculum research', in the book *Behaviour Modification in Education*, edited by C. E. Thorensen, published by N.S.S.E. Chicago in 1973; and more recently, Fry, L., 'Remedial Reading using a Home-based Token Economy' in the book *Parental Involvement in Children's Reading*.) Using prizes as well as praise has been found effective in strengthening reading accuracy (but not necessarily comprehension). The approach is to give rewards little and often, or to give the child points for words he reads correctly, and which he can later exchange for something he wants (like sweets or small privileges). The praise and feedback element of paired reading has the same kind of beneficial effect, and with practice is easier and more natural to use than prizes or points.

Pause, Prompt and Praise
(See Glynn, T., McNaughton, S. S., and Robinson, V. R., 'Remedial Reading at Home: Helping you to help your Child', New Zealand Council for Educational Research 1979.)

This technique aims to encourage the child to use various clues (such as the meaning of the story, or the look of the word) to get words right. It concentrates on the parent helping the child in different ways, depending on the kind of mistake he has made. As in paired reading, the parent pauses to give the child a second try at a problem word, and praises him for getting words right. There is however no reading together; instead, when the child is stuck he is prompted in one of three basic ways. If he cannot try the word at all, he must read the rest of the sentence to see if he can find a clue to what the word is (if this doesn't work, he is told the answer). If he makes a mistake that makes a nonsense of the sentence, the parent prompts him with clues about the meaning of what he is reading. If his mistake does make sense (the word fits the story, but is not the word printed on the page), then prompting concentrates on what the word looks like. From the discussion of the clues that help to identify words in Chapter One, it can be seen that Glynn and McNaughton's technique is to encourage the child to use certain ways of working words out (picking up the clues) rather than others (like concentrating on sounding all the problem words out).

The research on Pause, Prompt and Praise so far is encouraging, and good improvements in reading have been reported. Most 'PPP' projects reported have however needed more frequent supervision to be given to parents (weekly or twice-weekly) than is needed for paired reading, because the technique is rather more complicated.

Precision Teaching

This is a very detailed teaching technique, but it is one that a few schools have introduced to parents to use at home. Basically, a very precise 'chunk' of reading skill (like being able to recognize a list of difficult nouns) is broken down into small steps which are systematically taught, with clear targets to be achieved and objective measurements of progress. The teaching is carefully adjusted according to daily measurements of how the child is doing.

Precision teaching has not yet been fully evaluated with large groups of children, but it has been found very helpful to a number of individual children, and it has been used in home/school projects. Clearly, it is a technique that parents and teachers need to be specially taught to use.

SPECIAL READING BOOKS

There are basically two types of special books for children to read. Firstly is the whole range of ordinary children's books, containing stories or non-fiction suitable for children of various ages. Children's books differ from adults' books in having a simpler text, usually more illustrations, and often larger print. For younger children, there are few words per page, and

97

traditionally each page carries a picture plus a short piece of text.

Secondly, there are books specially written to help children with their reading. These include the school 'reading schemes' we are all familiar with. These scheme books (often numbered or colour coded) usually form a series of similar books of increasing difficulty so that the child can move from one to the next as his reading skills develop. Many introduce new words very carefully, and often include lists of new words or exercises for the child to do to help seal in what is new in each book. The advantage of having books in a series of increasing difficulty is that you can usually move the child to a slightly more difficult book at the right time (or back to a slightly easier one if needs be). A disadvantage is that reading scheme books are not usually very interesting – not many children would ever ask for one as a Christmas present! (It is very difficult for any author to write exciting stories when every sentence has to fit a particular level of difficulty, or he has to use only the words that have been 'revealed' by the story so far.) Another disadvantage is that every child on a reading scheme knows exactly how good or bad he is at reading. The child left on Book 1A when his mates are on 2A knows he is already a failure – and he will very quickly become anti-reading. Don't kid yourself that children are ever fooled by efforts to disguise which book comes where on schemes – they can see from the texts themselves who can't cope with more difficult reading – and will make sure he knows they know.

'Puddle Lane' Books

Another type of book specially intended for parents and children to read together at home is increasingly coming onto the market, with the growing popularity of parents helping children read. An example is the Ladybird 'Puddle Lane Reading Programme' written by Sheila McCullagh. Like the well-known 'Key Words' reading scheme, this includes books of progressively greater difficulty. The easier books have two versions of the story, plus pictures, printed side-by-side. One is for the adult to read to the child, the other is a simplified version for the child to read afterwards. With the more advanced books, the story is only printed once, but the right hand pages are easier than the left hand ones. With these the parent reads the book aloud first, then parent and child read it together, the parent reading the left pages, the child the right hand ones. The series finishes with a final stage in which the child should cope with both sides of the page once he has heard his parent read the book first.

'Read Along' Stories

These, published by Cambridge University Press, follow a similar idea. Again, they form a series of carefully increasing difficulty, each page having a simple version of the story for the child and a fuller version for the parent to read, plus pictures. This time the simpler version is given in comic-style 'speech bubbles' on the pictures. Simple speech bubbles plus a more difficult text beneath can be found in many children's books and comics. With this series, an adult reads the text to the child, the child tries the 'bubble version' and the bubbles contain only words from a list of the words most commonly used in children's reading schemes.

'Paired Reading Storybooks'

This series, written by Bill Gillham and published by Methuen, is also intended for very young children just beginning to read. With paired reading, the child can cope with whatever words he comes across, without having to be limited to the words already introduced (as in the 'gradually more difficult' type of reading scheme). The author aims to exploit this freedom to use whatever words fit the story best, with the intention of making the books more interesting to the child.

Each book in this series contains a set of instructions for doing paired reading. These instructions, however, are not for the full paired reading technique but are for the variation of it described earlier in this chapter.

CONCLUSION

There are now variations and alternatives available to paired reading. Many of these share common elements, and many have good results as shown in research studies. A review of various approaches has been undertaken by Keith Topping, an educational psychologist running a government-funded paired reading project in Kirklees ('Which Parental Involvement in Reading Scheme? A guide for practitioners', Paired Reading Project, Kirklees Education Department 1985). This (gratifyingly!) recommends paired reading as I first introduced it in the mid 1970's (and as it is described in this handbook) as the 'best buy'. This is on the basis of 'massive evidence from 50 published studies' and better results in improving both accuracy and comprehension than the variations and alternatives. Topping also notes that in six research studies which compared paired reading with other techniques, paired reading came out best in two and at least as good as the other techniques in the other four studies. More specific research results on paired reading's effectiveness are given in the next chapter.

On special reading schemes, it should be stressed that such books are no more, nor less, suitable for use when paired reading than any other children's book in the bookshop. Schemes that become progressively more difficult are better for good or average readers than they are for poor readers. With poor readers, they all hit the problem that the child's tastes and interests in reading matter go on progressing beyond the simple books he gets left behind on. For the very young, Gillham's 'storybooks' are not restricted to few and simple words because the child will have a form of paired reading help – but other young children's books which are not part of reading schemes are also free of limited vocabularies. With the extensive use of paired reading, there is no reason why numerous children's authors shouldn't continue to write for very young children using quite adventurous vocabularies.

The final word on special books needs to be a reminder – *You can use paired reading with any type of book: there is no need to buy any special books or reading schemes.*

EIGHT: SUCCESSES AND FAILURES OF PAIRED READING

In commending the readers of this handbook to try using paired reading because it has been found effective with large numbers of children already, it is important for me to refer to some of the research reports that have been produced on how effective it really is. That is the purpose of this chapter.

The vast majority of the research studies that have been done have been undertaken by psychologists and teachers quite independently of both myself and the colleagues with whom I first worked on paired reading. This is important in establishing the credibility of the results: one should always be rather sceptical of claims made for any technique when they all come from its originator! Paired reading, however, has been subjected to more research investigation than most educational techniques. What is very encouraging, both for myself and for anyone checking whether the technique is likely to work for their child, is that the different results reported by numerous different researchers are remarkably consistent in showing good results from paired reading.

Methods of Evaluation
The way some research studies are designed gives stronger evidence about the effects of paired reading than is produced by other studies. There can be no such thing as absolute proof that all the improvements children showed in reading were caused by paired reading – and as any researcher should beware, even the best of results could *just* be a fluke! The following factors are the main ones that make it likely that good

results are produced by paired reading and not by any chance or fluke:

a) similar results coming from a number of different and quite independent studies;

b) studies involving large numbers of children;

c) good results coming from studies which compared the progress of a group of children doing paired reading with that of a group of *similar* children not doing paired reading (this checks that the children were not going to improve in reading anyway, regardless of paired reading). This is the famous 'control group' type of study that is so important in testing techniques out, whether in education or in other fields such as the effects of medicines;

d) different studies reporting similar results despite using different ways of measuring the children's progress in reading. Many studies have used one particular reading test – the Neale Analysis of Reading Ability – but the fact that some paired reading studies have used other tests and produced good results eliminates the possibility that paired reading may be producing children good at doing that particular test without improving in their general reading skills!

The studies described briefly in this chapter include those involving large groups of children, those particularly convincing studies that followed the vital 'control group' design without which one should never make too many claims about any technique, and those that used reading tests and measures other than the popular Neale test. I have not included every study that has been done on paired reading; I keep hearing of new ones, and have found it quite impossible to keep abreast of those that are under way in various parts of this country and abroad. I have included information on where the original research reports can be found, partly to 'declare my sources', and partly for the benefit of the reader who may wish to carry out a paired reading research project himself or herself, and who needs far more detail than I have given.

THE RESEARCH RESULTS

The first two studies on paired reading were the ones I published in 1976 ('Paired Reading Tuition – a preliminary report on a technique for cases of reading deficit', in *Child Care Health and Development*, volume 2, pages 13–28) and, with Elizabeth Lyon, in 1979 ('Paired Reading – a preliminary report on a technique for parental tuition of reading-retarded children', in the *Journal of Child Psychology and Psychiatry*, volume 20, pages 151–160). In the first, I tried paired reading out as a new technique with three children, doing all the tuition myself, and found that the children's reading accuracy, reading comprehension, and (for the two where I could measure this over the whole period of the study) percentage of words read correctly all improved. In the second, we taught the new technique to parents to use with four children of junior school age, and found that over a period of six months in which we did one three- month course of paired reading, the children's average reading ages improved eleven and three quarter months for reading accuracy and eleven and a half months for reading comprehension. They also enjoyed paired reading into the bargain! As their titles suggest these studies were very small and could not prove that paired reading alone was responsible for the children's improvements. They did however show that paired reading was something worth trying out further, that it held good promise, and that it could be done by parents. Other researchers now began to check these early results out in other parts of the country, and to put paired reading very testingly through its paces before recommending its more widespread use.

The first control group study of paired reading was done by Heath (who reported it as 'A Paired Reading Programme' in *Edition 2*, the journal of the Inner London Education Authority School Psychological Service, in 1981 – pages 22–32). This was paired reading's acid test; Heath compared the progress of nineteen children after a three month course of paired reading, with that of sixteen children who did not do paired reading. The average age of the children was 7. The only difference between the two groups' experiences was paired reading itself. The children who had done paired reading improved in their reading accuracy at twice the normal rate, and in their reading comprehension at three and a half times the normal rate — in both cases, this was far better than the children who did not do paired reading. Heath commented that this 'evidence for the effectiveness of the whole procedure is fairly unequivocal, and shows gains which are unlikely to have been made by availing the children of traditional remedial provisions'.

Since then, paired reading has been found effective in other control group studies. Robson, Miller and Bushell reported that children doing paired reading did significantly better in both improving their reading accuracy and the comprehension of what they were reading than children not doing paired reading ('The development of paired reading in High Peak and West Derbyshire', published in *Remedial Education*, 1984, volume 19, pages 177–183). This was a large study involving fifty-four children, and is particularly convincing because in it children tried paired reading in many cases after already doing less well in a control group without it, and because people testing the children's progress did not know whether the children they were testing had been doing paired reading or not. Spalding, Drew and Ellbeck, also writing in the journal *Remedial Education* in 1984 ('If you want to improve your reading, Ask your Mum', in volume 19, pages 157–161), found a less impressive result when they compared the progress of sixteen children aged 11 and 12 doing a variant of paired reading, with that of a control group of sixteen children not receiving this help at home. The children receiving the special help progressed far better than the others in their comprehension of what they read, but no more than the others in the accuracy of their reading. However, in this study paired reading had been changed so that the parent started reading together with the child, but then faded her reading out to leave the child reading alone as the same passage of the book was read and re-read. This is not therefore a failure of paired reading as described in this book – but underlines the moral that varying the technique may vary the results that are produced.

In the book *Parental Involvement in Children's Reading* that has already been referred to in Chapter Seven, a control group study by Carrick-Smith is published. This involved twenty-eight children doing paired reading and twenty-eight 'control group' children for comparison, aged 12 and 13, from three schools. There were wide differences between individual children's progress after a six week paired reading course, but on average the children doing paired reading with their parents improved at three times the normal rate in reading accuracy (compared with improvement at the normal rate only for the children not doing paired reading), and at six times the normal rate for comprehension (compared with two and a half times). These improvements lasted after paired reading had finished; but there were differences between schools in how well their children did on average. How the school works with parents over reading may well be an important factor in getting the best out of a home/school reading project.

In the *Paired Reading Bulletin* published by the Kirklees Psychological Service (Kirklees Metropolitan Council, West Yorkshire), in 1985, O'Hara reports better results for children doing paired reading than for control group children, in a study involving paired reading with twelve physically handicapped 5 to 11 year olds. In the same Bulletin there is one disappointing study reporting worse results than usual in these control group studies. Walsh and colleagues did not find major improvements in reading skills amongst eleven children doing paired reading when compared with another eleven children not doing this, although the paired reading children did improve greatly in their pleasure and interest in reading. The key problem was that because of language difficulties, most of the children's parents were unable to do paired reading with them, and older brothers and sisters or other volunteers were recruited to help instead. It has been found quite possible to produce good results with children who do not speak English as their first language at home, and also when people other than parents do the tuition (see Chapter Nine), but clearly one has to work harder and use extra strategies to achieve good results under these circumstances. Walsh and colleagues add the comment that they are now using the experience of this first project and are producing better results with other children in their school.

Another control group study of paired reading was carried out in Cleveland by Winter in 1984 ('A Short Term Paired Reading Workshop for Parents: a controlled study', carried out by the County of Cleveland Psychological Service, and to be published), in which the effects of the paired reading done by thirteen junior school children with their parents was worked out by comparing their progress with that of thirteen similar children not doing paired reading. The course of paired reading was unusually short (only four weeks), but still the paired reading led to improvements in the children's accuracy of reading of 4.9 months, and in their comprehension of 8.6 months (compared with three and a half months in accuracy and six months in comprehension for children in the control group).

One very small but also very interesting control group study recently published by Eileen Limbrick and colleagues ('Reading Gains for Underachieving Tutors and Tutees in a Cross-Age Tutoring Programme', in the *Journal of Child Psychology and Psychiatry*, 1985, volume 26, pages 939–953) monitored the reading progress of three 6 to 8 year old children who were doing paired reading with three *10 to 11 year old* tutors, and compared it with a control group of other children. A number of measures of progress were used, and paired reading was found to benefit the children involved (both as tutors and as tutees – the involvement of children as tutors for other children is discussed in the next chapter).

As a check on my own paired reading work, I conducted a control group study with seven children doing paired reading with their parents, and another eight children in the control group. To avoid the danger of influencing my own results, all the reading testing to measure progress was done by a psychologist who did not know which children had done paired reading. The paired reading children, on average, progressed 6.3 months in accuracy of reading after three months of tuition, and 9.3 months in comprehension, compared to progress of only two months in accuracy and no progress at all in comprehension for children in the control group not doing paired reading.

Moving on from the research studies that have been designed as experiments, with control groups, to put paired reading to the test, many reports have been written up describing successful paired reading projects carried out by various schools. These have usually involved parents tutoring their own children at home after being taught paired reading by school staff or educational psychologists. Some studies have involved people other than parents carrying out the tuition (including other children with better reading skills, or in an older age group). Examples of these reports are given in the next chapter.

Writing in the *Journal of the Association of Educational Psychologists*, in 1982, Bushell and his colleagues reported that after an eight week paired reading course, twenty-two children (average age 10) had improved an average of three times the normal rate in reading accuracy, and six and a half times in reading comprehension. Those with the worst reading problems to start with did just as well as those with lesser reading problems. ('Parents as Remedial Teachers', volume 5 of the Journal, pages 7–13.) In a paper produced by the Leeds Psychological Service in 1983, Pitchford and Taylor reported similarly encouraging results for sixty-two children aged 7 and 8, who in eight weeks of paired reading progressed three times that amount of time in accuracy and five times in comprehension. Even in a special school for children with learning difficulties, Topping and McKnight in 1984 reported eighteen 11 to 14 year olds to progress twice the normal rate for accuracy and six times the normal rate for comprehension. (The sources of these two studies are Pitchford and Taylor, 'Paired Reading, Previewing and Independent Reading', Leeds City Council Psychological Service, and Topping and McKnight, 'Paired Reading – and Parent Power', *Special Education: Forward Trends*, volume 11, pages 12–15.) Reports of school paired reading projects done by parents at home also appeared in the 1985 *Paired Reading Bulletin*, again showing good results. Simpson reported accuracy gains of three times normal and comprehension gains of six times normal on average for twenty-six children after a paired reading project, and with nine first year secondary school pupils Hodgson reported accuracy and comprehension gains of 2.3 and five times normal rates, respectively.

The picture that emerges from all these studies is that after a course of paired reading, with children from infant school up to teenagers and regardless of the child's level of reading difficulty to start with, one can reliably expect marked improvements in the child's accuracy and comprehension of reading. Normally, an improvement in the child's reading age for accuracy of reading of about three times the length of the paired reading course can be expected. Thus the average child doing paired reading is likely to gain about nine months in his accuracy reading age after a three months course. This is, of course, particularly good progress for a child with reading problems, because not only is it faster progress than normal, but even 'normal' progress has been a problem for the child in the past. The improvement in reading after paired reading has also been found when different reading tests and measures were used, and research with control groups has shown that the improvements can be credited to the paired reading rather than to chance or fluke. The research results are remarkably consistent in supporting paired reading's effectiveness. Far from paired reading simply improving the technicalities of reading, moreover, it is clear that it greatly improves the child's comprehension of what he is reading as well. Most studies show an even greater improvement in comprehension than in accuracy of reading.

One caution should however be sounded; while these results have been produced by paired reading courses of various lengths, one cannot expect the same rate of progress to keep on going over very long periods of continued paired reading. The progress is likely to level out eventually, and we do not yet know from the research that has been done, exactly when this is likely to happen.

Very many of the studies listed in this chapter and the next have reported the vital side effects of paired reading that were referred to in earlier chapters. Most have reported that the children and parents found it an enjoyable technique to do at home; in some cases this was reported after interviewing those involved, or asking parents and children to fill in questionnaires about how they had found the technique to be in practice. Most also reported that during and after paired reading, the children helped became more interested in reading, often began reading for themselves outside paired reading sessions, and gained in confidence. These improvements were in some cases reported as extending outside reading itself, so that the children became more positive in their attitudes and efforts in other school work, generally more confident in themselves, and even on occasions better behaved! A very common side effect to be reported was that children and parents doing paired reading together became closer to one another, as the result of a joint successful effort at something that mattered to both of them.

Paired reading has now been going long enough for some reports to have appeared covering a large number of projects in a given school or local education authority. Avril Bush has published the results of a number of projects at Deighton School in Yorkshire ('Paired Reading at Deighton Junior School', in the book *Parental Involvement in Children's Reading*, 1985), involving a total of eighty-six children who made impressive average gains of five and a half times normal for accuracy and eight and a half times normal for comprehension. Pitchford and Taylor, in another paper from the Leeds Psychological Service entitled 'Paired Reading in East Leeds' (1984) reported the expected level of average improvements in reading after courses of paired reading for 233 children in seventeen different schools. Significantly, sixteen of the seventeen schools definitely (and the other one possibly) wished to continue using paired reading after their first experience of it. By far the largest series of paired reading projects is being carried out in Kirklees, Yorkshire, where in his First Annual Report in 1985, the Project Leader of this Government sponsored scheme, Keith Topping, reports on the use of paired reading with 425 children in twenty-seven separate projects. Nine out of ten of these projects were fully evaluated, and the average improvements in the children's reading were three times the normal rate for reading accuracy and four times the normal rate of increase in reading age for comprehension. Of the twenty-seven projects, only two produced unsatisfactory results (and one of the reported problems here was industrial action going on in schools at the time, and organisational problems, rather than a failure of the children concerned to respond to paired reading).

Thus, reported research so far leads one to the conclusion that paired reading does improve most children's reading, and can be recommended for widespread use.

More research is being conducted by an increasing number of reading researchers. Many of the studies involved aim to test the usefulness of paired reading in different ways to the 'standard' use by parents working at home with their own children of junior, secondary, or (increasingly) infant school age. Amongst the studies shortly to be published are some using the technique to help mentally handicapped children, children having language problems affecting their reading, children tutoring other children, adults, and studies comparing paired reading with some of the variants and alternatives described in Chapter Seven.

NINE: WIDER USES OF PAIRED READING

Most of this book has been concerned with parents using paired reading with their own children at home. When I started paired reading off, I had not foreseen its wide use by parents – I saw it at the time as something for psychologists and teachers to use with children. After using adult volunteers to tutor other people's children, it seemd to be an obvious step to give the technique to parents to use, and it has now become a standard method for parents to help children read.

Since then, other ways of using paired reading have been developed. It has been used to help children who do not speak English as their mother-tongue, it has been used with very young children and with teenagers and it is starting to be tried out in helping adults with reading problems (it is not yet clear what the results of paired reading with adults will be). As well as being used to help children who find reading difficult, paired reading has also been used successfully to help children just starting school to learn to read, and even to boost the reading of children whose reading skills are already better than average. It has also been found very effective for children to use paired reading with each other. My purpose in this final chapter is to give a brief outline of these wider uses of paired reading, together with some thoughts of what may lie ahead. I have also included some comments on training people (parents, volunteers or other children) to use the technique.

Paired Reading with Very Young Children
In Chapter Seven some variations of paired reading, especially for very young children, were described. 'Normal' paired reading as described in this handbook is however quite suitable for children just starting school.

It is useful as a home-support to the reading teaching going on in the classroom (remembering that it does not 'clash' or interfere with other methods of teaching reading that are being used at the same time). The successful use of paired reading with 'starting readers' at infant school has been described by Jungnitz and her colleagues in a paper entitled 'The development and evaluation of a paired reading project' (in the *Journal of Community Education*, 1983, No 4 pages 14–22). A number of infant schools are now using paired reading.

In using paired reading with very young children, keeping the praise level high for any words the child manages is very important. Very young children can certainly pick up the idea of signalling you to stop (my younger daughter, just beginning to try to read, thinks thumping on the arm of the chair for me to stop reading is the best bit of the whole business!). The key with many beginning readers is to let them use a well known book if they want, even if they know it by heart. Stopping Mum or Dad to 'read' alone – and getting praised for it, when you know the book by heart – is a good introduction to the idea of paired reading. It does not matter that the child may not even be looking at the text at first, because he is 'reciting' it. Once the habit is established, it can soon be tried with a less familiar book (perhaps, initially, one that has only been read to the child once or twice before), and eventually with a new one.

Children whose Mother-Tongue is not English

There are many children learning to read in English, although their home-language is not English. Paired reading can be very successful with children in multi-cultural schools (see a chapter by A. M. Bush on 'Paired Reading at Deighton Junior School', in the book *Parental Involvement in Children's Reading*, 1985). The one major problem here is that the tutor helping the child needs to be reasonably able to read in English, and not all parents in multi-cultural settings have themselves been taught to read in English. Jungnitz (writing on 'A Paired Reading project with Asian families' in the same book), found good results by identifying various different people, often teenaged brothers or sisters, to do paired reading with Asian children in a primary school.

Paired Reading with Above Average Readers

In 1985, following a national conference on paired reading, a number of reports on paired reading projects in various parts of the country were collected together in the *Paired Reading Bulletin* (published by the Psychological Service of Kirklees Metropolitan Council). This contained three reports of paired reading in which children who were good readers to start with, improved their reading with paired reading help at home. B. Fawcett ('The Cowersley Junior School Paired Reading Project') found that on average the eleven children taking part with their parents in his project improved their reading at four times the normal rate: and they were on average one year and four months ahead of normal in their reading to start with. In another project (at Kayes First and Nursery School, written up in the same 1985 *Bulletin*), the same kind of thing happened with twenty-four infant school children in a very 'well-off' village. Their reading improved at two and a half times the normal rate – and even at their young age they were already on average a year ahead of their actual ages for reading, before paired reading started. In the third project (by P. Bruce; 'Paired Reading with Mixed Ability Middle Infants'), average and above-average readers did just as well on paired reading as those who needed help with reading.

Perhaps it is not surprising that people are beginning to find that paired reading can be helpful to good readers as well as those with difficulties. It is however very important that it seems paired reading might give a boost in reading skill to good readers too. The message is that if you want to help your child with reading, however good or bad his reading is at present, paired reading is worth a try.

Children Tutoring other Children

Reports have begun to appear of projects in various schools in which children have done paired reading with other children. In some of these 'peer tutoring' projects, good readers helped poor readers of the same age (see S. Winter and A. Low, 'The Rossmere Peer Tutor Project' published in 1984 in *Behavioural Approaches with Children* Vol 8, pp 62–65; two reports in the 1985 *Paired Reading Bulletin* – I. Gale and D. Kendall 'Working together: the Marsden Junior School Peer Tutor Project' and L. Free and colleagues 'Parent, Peer and Cross-age Tutors'). Other reports describe projects in which older children tutored younger children (see L. Carrick-Smith 'A research project in paired reading' in the book *Parental Involvement in Children's Reading*; and S. Cawood and A. Lee 'Paired Reading at Colne Valley High School', reported in the *Paired Reading Bulletin*). One study which has reported very good results for older children tutoring younger children is that by Eileen Limbrick and her colleagues in New Zealand ('Reading gain for under-achieving tutors and tutees in a Cross-Age tutoring programme' published in 1985 in the *Journal of Child Psychology and Psychiatry*, Vol 26 pages 939–953).

One might be forgiven for being worried that children tutoring other children would lead to all sorts of problems and that it would waste the time of the better readers doing the tutoring. (After all – a decade ago, the educational textbooks said that helping children with reading difficulties was a highly specialized job needing expert professionals to do it, and even I was worrying about parents being asked to do paired reading!) What has come out of these early reports is a very different – and much better – story. The results so far show that children needing help with reading (of junior or lower secondary school age) and tutored by other children, do improve in their reading. With training and supervision by their teachers, better readers make good tutors. What is even more encouraging is that the children themselves liked being tutored by other children.

The most encouraging result of all is that when children tutor other children of the same age, *the tutors' reading improves as well as that of the children they are tutoring.* If this result keeps repeating itself as it has so far, a whole range of possibilities opens up. It may be possible for better readers and poor readers to team up as a regular classroom activity, as a way of helping poor readers to cope and boosting the skills of the better readers at the same time. Provided the difference in reading ages is enough (perhaps two years), poor readers could themselves help younger poor readers – with a boost in confidence by doing so.

Children helping each other through paired reading looks very promising (particularly where, for one reason or another, a parent is not able to help). This is however still an area in its early stages, and I would advise any school interested in 'peer tutoring', firstly that it is worth trying on the basis of the reports to far, and secondly that the progress and views of *both* tutors and tutees amongst the children should be monitored.

Setting up a School Paired Reading Project

Many schools are now setting up paired reading projects. The precise organisation of the project depends on the individual school – for some schools, the project is a first venture into involving parents; for others, it is one of many joint ventures between home and school. The amount of staff time available to train people to do paired reading, and to supervise how they are doing it, is also important in deciding how to run the project.

The most successful projects are those in which there is good supervision after initial training in paired reading, in which class teachers are fully involved in following the scheme through (so that the project is not just an 'optional extra' tacked on to the 'real' business of the school), and where the parents are supported in continuing to encourage and help their children read after the project proper is over. A paired reading project is often a good 'booster' to reading in the school, and can be followed by either more use of paired reading itself by parents at home in the future, or by a more general form of reading support (see the section on 'after paired reading' below).

There are a number of key decisions about the type of paired reading project you want to run. The first is

117

whether you are intending to run a research project to investigate the value for your pupils of a variation on the already evaluated technique, or to monitor an aspect of reading which has not usually been monitored (such as changes in your pupils' attitudes to reading outside the project). If you are planning a straightforward project to help pupils read, rather than a piece of research, you then need to decide on the children you are going to involve. This will depend on your own priorities for reading work in the school, but may lead you to plan a project for the whole of an infants' class to accompany other work on reading being done in the classroom, or to work with junior or lower secondary school age children who have fallen behind in reading (eg by two years or more in reading age), or to give all children of say junior age, regardless of reading skill so far, a 'booster' in reading before they pass on to the next school. A secondary school may similarly aim to give children of its new intake a general reading boost. In selecting your 'target group' for paired reading, remember that you can combine paired reading with other standard or specialized reading techniques being used in the classroom or remedial unit without ill effects, and that the most reliably evaluated use of the technique is with children of junior or secondary age needing some help with their reading problems.

Having selected your target group of children to receive help, you need to choose your tutors for them. The most usual choice is the parents of the children themselves, but in some schools this choice may be affected by language differences, or by difficulties in 'recruiting' the parents to come to school to take on the role. In some cases, other family members or volunteers (such as other school staff – and not just the teachers) can be 'recruited' to help instead, and at least some home visits rather than all school-based training and supervision sessions may be necessary. Increasingly, however, it is worth considering a 'peer tutoring' project instead, in which the children will be tutored by other children in the school. This will be your choice if you have *two* target groups of children you want to help read, with reading ages at the outset ideally two years apart or more. Since the children doing the tutoring are likely to increase their reading skills as well (and on experience reported so far, they are likely to take their task very responsibly), your tutors may be average or better readers of the same age as the tutees, older children with reading problems themselves who can read better than the tutees, or older children without reading problems. Same-age peer tutoring has been done successfully in both junior and secondary schools, and the older tutors taking part in the reported 'cross age' projects have ranged from junior age children (tutoring infants successfully) to sixth formers.

Once both tutors and tutees have been identified, you need to decide on your method of training and monitoring. The basic choice here is between training and supervising each 'pair' of child and tutor individually, or working with them as a group. The staff time you have available may make your choice for you, since individual training is very time consuming. My own preference is for individual training of each 'pair', since this allows the adjustment of the training to suit the individual tutor and child and produce high levels of proficiency early on. With group training, there is always the danger of the tutor who leaves the sessions not quite having grasped what to do. A sound compromise is to arrange group training, but to allow for some pairs to be individually trained if they really prefer, or if they do not pick the technique up easily in the group sessions.

However you decide to do the training, it is essential that you do provide adequate supervision afterwards, while the tutors are actually doing paired reading with the children – for all the reasons set out earlier in this book. Fortnightly supervision and monitoring sessions should be regarded as the minimum. These can certainly take place at school (provided the timing suits the tutors) rather than needing home visits, and can be group sessions at least (though to deal with the specific advice that most will need, individual supervision is better). If you do not have the resources to carry out this minimum

119

level of supervision, it is very doubtful whether you should be launching a project at all.

There is no fixed rule about the best duration of a school paired reading project, and it is likely that much of the benefit will be seen fairly early on, when the children are showing the effects of improved attitudes towards reading. A three month period would be an appropriate length for most projects (assuming a quarter of an hour's paired reading on most days). Some schools have however found good results with six week projects, or even in some cases a shorter time than this.

Any school undertaking a paired reading project should monitor both its effectiveness for the children concerned (as described in Chapter Five), and, for future reference, its practicalities.

Training the Tutors
Whether you are training your paired reading tutors individually or in groups, the children on the receiving end of the tuition will need training in what they are supposed to be doing. In training tutor/child 'pairs' individually, the child is automatically taught what to do by the person doing the training. This trainer will need to show the would-be tutor the various stages of the technique, demonstrating them with the tutor's own child. In training tutors in groups, there needs to be a carefully supervised stage when the tutors being trained in the group begin working with their own children.

Individual training of tutors can follow broadly the stages set out in Chapter Four on how to start doing paired reading. At each stage, the trainer should introduce the child to the procedure, then demonstrate it to the trainee tutor, who will then try it with the child (with prompting and advice from the trainer).

I normally expect to spend one to one and a half hours in training each tutor/child pair individually from scratch – usually in two three quarter hour sessions. Two tips may be helpful. Firstly, encourage the child to use a fairly easy book (of his choice) during the first stages of training, so that he is likely to give his tutor some practice at coping with signals that he wants to read alone. Secondly, teach tutor and tutee to read effectively together by reading aloud with them yourself before asking them to do it as a pair. Reading as a threesome lets the tutor learning the ropes pick up the reading together technique from the model you are providing of how to do it. This is similar to the way the child will be picking up correct reading from the tutor's 'model' later on.

In individual training, the child usually picks up what to do extremely quickly – so even a child totally new to paired reading can demonstrate what to do to his future tutor almost immediately, provided that he is working with an experienced trainer. The three most difficult parts of paired reading for new tutors to learn are to keep up the praise/feedback, to remember how to respond when the child signals, and to remember the 'four second rule'. I usually ask the new tutor to try the whole technique very early on, but to rely on me prompting her on how to respond to signals and the child making mistakes or getting stuck, until she has got the hang of it all. I usually find that I have to give a lot of prompting to give praise at first, before this begins to come naturally.

When training children as tutors for other children, it is tempting to try to simplify paired reading to help the child-tutors out. This is not necessary. Child tutors have been found quite capable of coping with full paired reading. Two tips that may help in training on a peer tutoring project are, firstly, to allow the children who are going to be tutored to choose their own tutors from those available on the project before training begins, and secondly, to think carefully about the terminology to be used on the project. Will the term 'partner' be better than 'tutor' in your same-age project, for example, and is the term 'feedback' more acceptable than 'praise'?

Many schools using a group approach to training tutors have started off by demonstrating how *not* to hear a child read (no praise, plenty of criticism, and demands to 'sound' everything out whenever it is difficult). This is usually done with the help of a video recording of staff acting the roles of tutor and child, or by staff doing this

121

'role-playing' live to the group (depends how uninhibited your staff are!). By 'hamming it up' a bit, this can be a useful ice-breaker for the group – even if many parents will find the demonstration of what not to do uncomfortably familiar! After explaining things, the well-tried format of group training usually proceeds to a demonstration of the stages of paired reading. This may be done by using a video of paired reading being done, by a trainer demonstrating things with a volunteer child to the group, or again by two trainers role-playing.

Many people ask trainee tutors to practise paired reading (or the various parts of it as they are taught) with each other, before trying it out with the child they are going to work with after training. This can however be a little embarrassing for adults learning the technique – especially if you've failed to get the group really relaxed with each other first. It is better in many cases to bring the children concerned in at this stage (after explaining and demonstrating what is to be done), and to ask each pair to practise paired reading together with the training staff checking carefully how each new tutor/child pair is doing, and giving individual help wherever needed. After group training, it is important to arrange a first supervision session with everybody very soon after they have started paired reading on their own with their children, to pick up and deal with any problems before they can get a hold.

Whether your training has been individually done for each 'pair', done in a group, with parents, volunteer tutors, or other children as 'peer tutors', it is helpful to send each tutor 'solo' with a written reminder of what to do, to refer to as necessary. The summary of paired reading on page 65 gives a basis for this, which can be adapted to suit your particular age group of tutor and local requirements (eg to include arrangements about supervision, or where to get books locally).

In order to train tutors, it is necessary for the staff doing the training to have successful experience of doing paired reading themselves. If there is no-one with this experience in your school, each member of staff who is going to train tutors should teach himself or herself to do paired reading first with one or two children, before the main project. It would also be wise to practise training a volunteer tutor of the right type (that is, a parent, other adult, or child) before taking on a group training session or a series of individual training sessions. Ironing out the problems and becoming familiar with both tuition itself and with the training of tutors before launching on the project, will pay dividends later in the smooth running and success of the school's project. I hope that this book will provide the guidance needed for school staff to teach themselves to do paired reading before teaching it to the tutors on a school-based project.

After Paired Reading

If you are a parent doing paired reading with your own child at home, the decision on whether to keep on going with it after you have done a reasonable initial period (of, say, three months) should depend on whether your monitoring of the child's progress (see Chapter Five) shows that he is improving his reading, or not. If he is improving his reading on paired reading, it is well worth carrying on while the 'winning streak' lasts. Keep monitoring progress, and have a break from regular sessions if progress stops, or if he stops enjoying paired reading. The last thing you should do at this stage is to risk putting him off reading again by pushing him to keep going for too long. After doing paired reading for the length of time you had initially decided upon (such as the fairly standard three months stint), and if progress merits carrying on, decide whether to press straight on with regular daily sessions, or whether to take a break of a month or so before starting again. It is far better to take a break and then have another 'course' of paired reading, than to let things drift on and finally peter out.

With many children, but not all, there will come a time when the child no longer seems to need paired reading help as such. The signs of this are the child being able to cope with most books appropriate to his age, spending most of each session reading alone rather than together, and signalling you to stop reading with him after only one word together each time you need to help him. At the same time, the child will be reading books and other reading material for himself, quite apart from paired reading or school requirements. Children who have begun to do this are truly choosing to read for their own pleasure – which is, after all, a major reason for teaching people to read in the first place.

When a child has reached this level of reading competence, you can do one of three things. You can stop all extra reading help, and remain ready to help again if the child does not maintain progress with reading in the future. Secondly, you can use paired reading with more advanced books still, to stretch his reading skills even further, or thirdly, you can put your help with reading on a 'care and maintenance' basis to keep the support and encouragement going without doing full paired reading.

In using paired reading as an advanced boost to reading, with books the child wants to read but which are beyond his new reading level (and which are perhaps in advance of his age group), there are a few warnings to be given. Firstly, *don't* push the child to keep going on to more difficult books if he doesn't *really* want to or if he is not enjoying it. There is a real risk otherwise that you will put him off reading again if you do this. Furthermore, *do* stop when he wants to stop, and only keep going with books in advance of his actual age if it is clear from proper monitoring that his reading skill is still improving. The key is to stop when either the enjoyment or the progress stops. These points are particularly important if you are using paired reading to boost the reading skills of a child whose reading to start with is already average or above average. Keeping your own monitoring going is absolutely essential in these circumstances, because far less is known from research work about paired reading with average or above average readers, than about paired reading with children of poor reading ability.

If you wish to put your reading help on a care and maintenance basis, replace paired reading sessions with regular, but less frequent, 'support sessions'. These may be tried perhaps twice a week to start with, reducing to once a week later on. Again, it is better to make a positive decision with the child to do this, than to soldier on with full paired reading after you have finished a standard 'course' of it, and then finding that everything simply peters out. In these 'support sessions', let the child read silently to himself while you are in the room (ideally, you can be reading your own book – or newspaper or office paperwork – at the same time!). Agree with the child that you will do paired reading together on some sections of his book – say every third page – to check how he is doing and to give a little tuition on the book to keep him 'topped up'. If he is coping well with the book, you will discover this, and your paired reading pages will be spent mostly with him reading alone but aloud to you. If he has ventured onto a difficult book which presents him with problems, he will have the benefit of learning some of the tricky words in the usual way, and you will have the benefit of knowing exactly how he is doing. When it becomes clear that he no longer needs your support in this way (he will eventually find it tedious to have to read the odd page aloud), the support sessions can be phased out. It is still worth reminding him that if he ever wants to try a particularly difficult book (perhaps one to do with a complicated hobby), he should not avoid it, but can ask you to paired read it with him as necessary.

With an older child in the family who has been helped by paired reading but who no longer requires such help, it is worth considering asking him to act as the paired reading tutor for a younger brother or sister. Remember that the evidence so far suggests that this is likely to boost the older child's reading as well, and it will certainly ease the load of tuition on the parents.

After a school paired reading project, it is important to be very clear to parents on what you want them to carry on doing to support reading at home. The advice to carry on paired reading, or to have a complete break before another bout of paired reading, or to give support as just described, or simply to encourage and give children the opportunities (and trips to the library) to carry on reading for themselves, should depend on each 'pair's' response and progress during the project. It is important when running a peer tuition project within the school, not only to explain it to the parents (who are quite justifiably likely to have initial misgivings otherwise about children tutoring each other in reading), but also to be clear on what you want the parents themselves to do at home. Having used paired reading and other home/school reading schemes to bring parents actively into their children's education, it is the school's duty to make its policy on the parents' involvement perfectly plain at each stage – and not just to forget the home/school link again once the school has 'done' its project.

The Future

Paired reading has come a long way in the last ten years, and some of its likely future developments are already becoming clear. I anticipate much more development of peer tutoring within schools, and of paired reading in the infant school as an aid to the initial learning of reading. Already, interest is growing in its use with handicapped children, and one looks forward to more research on this area – particularly on the possibilities of paired reading with mentally handicapped children and adults. Perhaps the two biggest potential areas for development are those of paired reading with children of normal reading ability to start with – as a general 'booster' to reading progress, and of paired reading with adults on adult literacy schemes. Both these areas need much more research work done upon them before the usefulness (or otherwise) of the approach with these groups of tutees can be more clearly stated.

There is likely to be more research work done too on the usefulness of various ways of 'delivering' paired reading, trying to answer questions such as: what is the best duration of a course of paired reading? Does most of the benefit happen in the early stages or is it more evenly spread over time? For how long will reading keep on improving if paired reading is continued over a long period (and is this different for children with reading problems to start with, compared with children of average or above average reading skills to start with)? Will a child usually improve his reading skills as much on a second course of paired reading as he does on the first one, or does the benefit wear off with each successive course? We are still not clear on what happens to a child's reading after he has finished a course of paired reading and gone back to normal school work on reading. Does he tend to fall behind again, or progress at a fairly normal rate without further special help once he has made up lost ground during paired reading? Perhaps the most important question of all is why some children do *not* either like or progress with, paired reading, and what can best be done at home to help them. They may be a minority, but they may have a more specialized need for help.

A pet hope of mine for the future is that someone will develop a 'standardized' reading test that can be used as a 'progress book' as was mentioned in Chapter Five. Standardized reading tests are good in that they allow you to compare your child's score with what is normal at his age, so that you can work out his reading age – but bad in that you cannot give the test every week to keep a constant check on progress. Using a progress book is good in that you can get the child to dip into it every week to check progress – but bad in that this only tells you whether he is improving or getting worse, and does not allow you to work out his reading age. What would be ideal would be a set of books suitable for each age group of children, each book being the same level of difficulty throughout and with the normal percentage of errors made by children of each age known so that reading ages could be calculated.

So far, paired reading has been used to improve children's reading. Remembering that I once did reading together with a child to help with his stammer and wondered what that was doing to his reading, I now wonder what doing paired reading to help with reading may be doing for the child's learning of the contents of what he is reading. We already know that paired reading produces a significant increase in children's comprehension of what they are reading. It would be interesting to 'paired read' something one wanted to learn by heart, as a way of learning it. The same technique would apply. Already a mother and child I am working with have decided to try 'paired tables' as a way of learning multiplication tables, and what about using the technique of paired reading to learn by heart a passage of poetry or one's lines for the school play? Again, what about using paired reading to learn the correct pronunciation of a foreign language from a fluent speaker? (Research students in search of topics for theses, please take note!) The same concepts of 'performing' together, signalling when able and confident to try continuing alone, and then 'performing' alone with praise or feedback, can also be applied to other skills than reading. The approach can be adapted to produce 'paired music', for example. These possibilities are fascinating, and many may wish to try them (remembering that there are no research reports on any of these yet, and therefore that one would be breaking new ground – although these approaches to learning together with someone more skilled all rest on various elements which are far from new or untried).

By far the most important future for paired reading is however that it should continue to be used, both by parents and in schools, to help children read. Developments and variations may be interesting and have good potential, but paired reading in its original form, as set out in this handbook, is well tried, safe, usually enjoyable, usually effective, and is used and recommended by very many people in the field of education other than myself. I hope that this book will have helped more children to read, and that it will have given more parents and schools a technique they find helpful.